AF540243

TEACHING–LEARNING BEHAVIOUR THROUGH SOFT KNOWLEDGE

TEACHING–LEARNING BEHAVIOUR THROUGH SOFT KNOWLEDGE

Edited by

Dr. S.K. Panneer Selvam

Assistant Professor
Department of Education
Bharathidasan University
Tiruchirappalli
Tamil Nadu
(India)

DISCOVERY PUBLISHING HOUSE PVT. LTD.
NEW DELHI-110 002

Published by:

Tilak Wasan

DISCOVERY PUBLISHING HOUSE PVT. LTD.

4383/4B, Ansari Road, Darya Ganj

New Delhi-110 002 (India)

Phone : +91-11-23279245, 43596064-65

Fax : +91-11-23253475

E-mail : parul.wasan@gmail.com

discoverypublishinghouse@gmail.com

web : www.discoverypublishinggroup.com

***First Edition:* 2012**

ISBN: 978-93-5056-122-5

Teaching–Learning Behaviour Through Soft Knowledge

Printed at:

Shree Balaji Art Press

Delhi

Preface

This is a compiled edition. The very purpose of this edition is to make the students and the teachers know what is going on around them in the academic world. Tamil 'teaching-learning' World Wide Web has not grown well. It is not an inspiring and influential exercise even today. Unless it acquires a global relevance and dimension among the Tamil speaking community. It will not touch the sentiments of our brothren. I solicit the learned Tamil scholars, linguistic experts, teachers to work together involving all the latest e-centre for universal teaching-learning process. I earnest request all the interested scholars and institutions to co-operate and co-ordinate in farming a viable curriculum for the benefit of the foreign Tamil learners.

Computer and other related technical easy and interesting. When students to 'light and sound' they do not feel the class room a duce place. Learning becomes a hobby. If the information and communication technology is not available to the Tamil teaching institutions, the Tamil community especially the budding community will become a laughing stock. e-technology offers multi-level approach in teaching a subject. Students can immensely benefit from multi level approach which is possible only through technology. The present century is witnessing a rapid and through change than the past century. Minute by minute the whole world is impacted and influenced by constantly evolving computer technology computer was introduced in India in 1960. India has become a giant in computer software. Our young talents have contributed immensely. We can be proud of them and their skills. Taking advantage of this conducive atmosphere there should be useful changes in the trends of teaching-learning Tamil.

It is worth mentioning that a Tamil news paper on computer is in circulation. It is the pilot publication in India. No other language in India enjoys this privilege. We have to standardize the Tamil words used in the computer world. To do this Herculean task I earnestly appeal to all the experts in Tamil language and in e-technology to sit together to draw out a workable common minimum programme. It is essential and very important to know that in most of the developed countries the medium of teaching is mother tongue. Keep it in mind and move forward should be our life long endeavour. I acknowledge their whole hearted thanks again and again. This book provides an illuminations and in-depth analysis of modern technology's learning.

All the articles are taken from the INFITT website—who gave the eminent persons in the field of IT to UTHAMAM of world Tamil union. The very purpose of this edition is to make the students and the teachers know what is going on around them in the academic world. Even the entrepreneurs in the realm of education find it more beneficial. Some of the articles are modified or simplified versions. As the author I am not able to trace out and contact the resource persons who were helpful in bringing out this book. I acknowledge their whole hearted thanks again and again.

Contents

Preface

List of Contributors

1. Enhancing Learning of Tamil Language in a One-to-One Computing Environment 1
2. Teaching and Resource Building in Teacher Education 13
   Dr. Seetha Lakshmi
3. Use of Technology in Running a Tamil School in USA 26
   Ilango Meyyappan
4. A Study on the Role of Tamil Virtual University in Tamilteaching and Learning at Elementary Level 36
   Dr. Nirmala Devi, S
   Dr. Rajeswari, T
5. ICT for Tamil Education in Tamilnadu Current Challenges and Opportunities 44
   Prof. S. Balaji
6. Enhancing Activity based Tamil Teaching and Learning using Online Video Repositories: A Data Mining based Approach 52
   Dr. K. Vivekanandan
   Dr. V. Saravanan
   Mr. P. Ranjit Jeba Thangaiah
7. Open Educational Resources in the Context of Teaching and Learning of Tamil as the First Language 58
   Dr. N. Balasubramanian

8. Computer Aided Learning in Tamil Sentences 67
Dr. G. Singaravelu

9. Moodle: For Enhanced learning (Tamil language)...... 75
Ravishankar Somasundaram

10. Quality Analysis of Tamil Virtual University 84
S. Rajkumar

11. Moodle: A Tool for Tamil Teaching 90
K.Sarveswaran
Prof. V.Nagarajan

12. Morphological Generator for Tamil: A new data 98
driven Approach
Rekha R, Anand kumar M, Dhanalakshmi V, Rajendran S

13. FaceWaves : A Tamil Text to Video Framework 106
Madhan Karky, Ravi Varman

14. Context Based Information Search for Thirukural ... 114
N. Ilakiyaselvan

15. Computational Approaches for Learning 120
Inflections in Tamil
K. Rajan, V. Ramalingam, M. Ganesan

16. Conceptual Lexicon for Knowledge Representation 130
S. Rajendran

17. Noun Phrase Chunker using Finite State 142
Automata for an Agglutinative Language
Vijay Sundar Ram R, Sobha Lalitha Devi

18. Animated Sangathamizh Poems - E Learning 152
Arul Natarajan

19. Representation of Kinship in WordNet 158
S. Arulmozi

20. Role of Regular Expression (RE) in Morphological 170
Analysis
R. Shanmugam

21. Transliteration Schemes for Tamil to Roman and 174
Roman to Tamil Characters
Dr. S. Srinivasan

22. From Classical Tamil to Computational Tamil: A Perspective 184
Dr. A. Kumaran

23. Spell Checker for Tamil using Finite State Automata 192
Anitha, S. Pillai

24. Automated Processing of Census Forms in Tamil 200
Shashi Kiran, Rituraj, Suresh Sundaram, Swapnil Belhe, AG Ramakrishnan

25. Pattern based English-Tamil Machine Translation ... 211
S. Saravanan, Dr. A.G. Menon, Dr. K. Soman

26. Bilingual TTS for Tamil and English 219
AG Ramakrishnan, Vikram LR, Abhinava, ShivaKumar HR

Index 225

List of Contributors

1. **Dr. Seetha Lakshmi**
   Associate Professor, Asian Languages & Cultures *National Institute of Education, Singapore.*
2. **Ilango Meyyappan**
   Principal, California Tamil Academy, Fremont Branch, California, USA.
3. **Dr. Nirmala Devi, S**
   Dept.of Education, Institute of Advanced Study in Education, Chennai-15.
4. **Dr. Rajeswari, T**
   Research Fellow, ECOLE FRANCAISE, Pondicherry.
5. **Prof. S. Balaji**
   D.B. Jain College, Chennai-97.
6. **Dr. K. Vivekanandan**
   School of Management, Bharathiar University, Coimbatore.
7. **Dr. V. Saravanan,**
   Dr. N.G.P. Institute of Technology, Coimbatore – 641 048.
8. **Mr. P. Ranjit Jeba Thangaiah**
   Karunya University, Coimbatore – 641 114.
9. **Dr. N. Balasubramanian**
   Director, School of Distance Education, Bharathiar University, Coimbatore.
10. **Dr. G. Singaravelu**
    Reader, UGC—Academic Staff College, Bharathiar University, Coimbatore.

11. **Ravishankar Somasundaram**
12. **S. Rajkumar**

    ME Industrial Engineering Kumaraguru Engineering College, Coimbatore.
13. **K. Sarveswaran**

    Sri Lanka
14. **Prof. V. Nagarajan**

    India
15. **Rekha R , Anand Kumar M, Dhanalakshmi V.**

    Amrita Vishwa Vidyapeetham Coimbatore.
16. **Rajendran S.**

    Department of Linguistics, Tamil University, Thanjavur.
17. **Madhan Karky, T V Geetha & Ravi Varman**

    Department of Computer Science & Engineering College of Engineering Guindy, Anna University.
18. **N. Ilakiyaselvan**

    CEG Anna University, Chennai-25.
19. **K. Rajan**

    Dept of Comp. Sc. and Engineering.
20. **V. Ramalingam**

    Dept of Comp Sc.
21. **M.Ganesan**

    Centre of Advanced Studies in Linguistics, Annamalai University, Annamalainagar.
22. **S. Rajendran**

    Tamil University, Thanjavur.
23. **Vijay Sundar Ram R and Sobha Lalitha Devi**

    MIT Campus of Anna University,
    Chromepet, Chennai – 44.
24. **Arul Natarajan**
25. **S. Arulmozi**

    Dravidian University

26. R. Shanmugam

Madras University

27. Dr. S. Srinivasan

Scientific Officer, Computer Division Indira Gandhi Centre for Atomic Research, Kalpakkam-603102.

28. Dr. A. Kumaran

Microsoft Research India, Bangalore, India.

29. Anitha. S Pillai

Hindustan University

30. Shashi Kiran, Rituraj, Suresh Sundaram, Swapnil Belhe, AG Ramakrishnan

MILE Lab, Dept of Electrical Engineering,
Indian Institute of Science, Bangalore - 560 012.

31. S. Saravanan, Dr. A. G. Menon, Dr. K. Soman

Amrita Vishwa Vidyapeetham, Ettimadai, Coimbatore.

32. AG Ramakrishnan, Vikram LR, Abhinava, Shivakumar HR

Medical Intelligence and Language Engineering Laboratory, Department of Electrical Engineering,
Indian Institute of Science, Bangalore - 560012.

1

Enhancing Learning of Tamil Language in a One-to-One Computing Environment

ABSTRACT

In recent years, there seems to be an upward trend of Indian pupils entering primary one who take Tamil as their Mother Tongue but come from non-Tamil speaking home environments. Pupils are found to be unable to effectively communicate their ideas and opinions in the language. Some even express fear and anxiety when asked to communicate their ideas in Tamil. This paper presents how technology can be leveraged in a one-to-one computing environment to enhance learning of Tamil language. In this environment, there is an eclectic blend of mastery driven approaches as well as constructivist pedagogies. In a ubiquitous computing environment, the teacher is able to tailor lessons and support pupils of varying abilities; thus scaffolding their learning to build their esteem and to eventually help them to gain confidence to communicate their ideas. This paper will show the strategies used in a technology-rich environment and the challenges faced by the Primary one and two classes to achieve the objectives.

Keywords: *Integration of Technology, One-to-one computing.*

Introduction & Purpose

Recent statistics shows that there is a shift of Tamil language usage at home (Ministry of Education—Singapore, 2005). The survey data findings conducted in our school with Tamil pupils during the Primary 1 orientation in 2008 and 2009 also reflected similar trend with close tc more than 40% of Tamil pupils coming from non-Tamil speaking background. This implied a lack of authentic context of the usage of the Mother Tongue languages at home. As a result pupils faced communication problems both in written and oral presentation of ideas, constructing a grammatically correct sentence and using the language in a particular situation or context. With a greater emphasis in Standard Spoken Tamil pupils are challenged further in the appropriate contextual usage of Tamil language.

Background of One to One Computing Environment

The school in this research study is Beacon Primary School, one of the future schools under the Future Schools @ SG project jointly initiated by the local Ministry of Education (MOE) and the Infocomm Development Authority (IDA). Its primary purpose is to explore the possibilities of using and leveraging on Information Communication Technologies (ICT) in the educational realm, especially in the area of Mother Tongue languages acquisition among young learners, aged 7 to 8. With this context in mind, series of lessons were designed and implemented emphasis on language building authentic activities with elements of play leveraging on Information Communication Technologies (ICT). All Tamil pupils were given a laptop and are equipped with basic handling of the equipment. All Tamil pupils are taught how to use Microsoft Power Point, Microsoft Word and Photostory 3 for Windows. The Tamil classroom is equipped with Promethean Interactive Whiteboard.

Studies have shown that ICT could be used to better engage learners (Fontana, Dede, White, & Cates, 1993;

Herrington & Oliver, 1998; Jonassen, Peck, & Wilson, 1999; Sarapuu & Adojaan, 1999; Oliver & Hannafin, 2000; Jonassen, 2000; Jonassen & Carr, 2000; Hollingworth & McLoughlin, 2001; Kearney & Treagust, 2001; Neo & Neo, 2001). Jonassen and Carr (2000) propose the approach of learning with technology where learners are actively involved in the construction of their own knowledge with the help of ICT tools.

They propose that technologies could be used as mind tools for the construction of their knowledge and engaging learners in evaluating, analysing, connecting, elaborating, synthesising, imagining, designing, problem-solving, and decision-making. ICT tools allowed learners to express their thought processes through multimedia presentations, that is, a consolidation of images, text, animation, and sound. Van Scoter (2004) advocates that digital images support language development. When young learners use ICT tools to tell stories they create with a combination of words and pictures, these stories present a wonderful opportunity for students to create an image with meaning for them. Haugland (1992) advocates that children using computers could gain intelligence, structural knowledge, long-term memory, manual dexterity, verbal skills, problem solving, abstraction and conceptual skills over those who did not use computers. The main idea is not to use the computer for itself but to include supporting activities that will allow for meaningful learning.

Rationale, Approach and Design

Rationale

Learning in complex and ill-structured knowledge domains requires accommodation of multiple perspectives embedded in authentic activities and the reconciliation of those perspectives with personal beliefs resulting in conceptual change. We reason that instead of merely flooding the pupils with vocabulary from anywhere, we are constructing knowledge and context through authentic activities. The authentic activities also included elements of play as a pedagogical tool.

Approach

A case study approach was used in this study to look into how authentic activities with elements of play and leveraging on the use of ICT to better engage pupils in learning of Tamil language. A case study approach is being used to better understand the impact and potentials of the strategies used in this study. Case study research is not sampling research and it is also not the primary intent of this study to understand other cases. According to Stake (1995), it may be useful to try to select cases that are typical or representative of other cases, but a sample of one or a sample of just a few is unlikely to be a strong representation of others. The most important criterion of using case study as a research method is to maximise what we can learn from this instance.

Design

The lessons are designed based on the three concepts of authenticity, learning with technology, and play as discussed above. Students were engaged in an authentic setting by playing. Using the experience and resources built during play (*e.g.*, digital images and vocabulary), they created digital stories using ICT tools. A diagram depicting the basic lesson design flow and its stages is presented in Figure 1.1.

The pupils were provided platform to enrich vocabulary by tying literacy with context using ICT tools. Examples of this strategy include the using of digital images, e-books, and online resources to build and understand the set of vocabulary used in the theme. Students were prompted to discuss about the topic. Figure 1.2 and 1.3 depict the usage of Big Books and Interactive White Board to engage pupils in the initial stage of this lesson design.

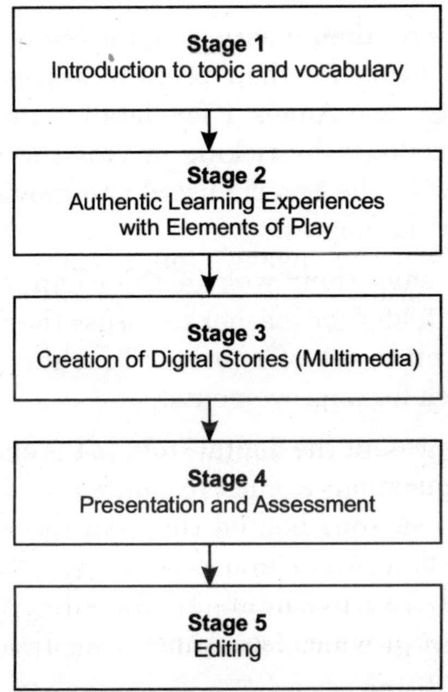

Fig. 1.1 : Lesson Design and Stages of Impika education

Stage1–Introduction to topic and vocabulary

Stage 2–Authentic Learning Experiences with Elements of Play

Pupils will go through an authentic experience or learning journey. These learning experiences help them internalise the information they gather and serve as a platform to verbalise their meaning making. Peer collaboration and interaction is a means for the pupils to articulate their thought processes.

Stage 3–Creation of Digital Story (Multimedia)

Using the resources accumulated during the authentic activity, pupils to create digital stories. These stories are the outputs of their authentic learning experience.

Stage 4–Presentation & Assessment

Pupils can present their creations in the following ways:

(a) Pupils save their creations in the computer network shared folder for their peers to assess based on a checklist (see Annex 1 for details). Peers to write their feedback by ticking or crossing appropriate boxes with the criteria listed and provide feedback to their classmates.

(b) Pupils save their wok in the computer network shared folder for teacher to assess the digital story based on a set of rubrics. Teachers to provide feedback for improvements.

(c) Pupils present the digital story to the class. Teacher to ask questions to elicit response from the pupils to explain reasons behind the text, images or audio recorded. Teacher and peers to give feedback for further improvements to the story based on a checklist provided (see Annex 1 for details).

Stage 5—Editing

Pupils take ownership in learning by editing after feedback was given by peers or teacher. Depending on the time frame, students may edit as many times as they want.

Research Methods

Pupils' Performance

A diagnostic test was conducted at the start of academic term to assess the reading, listening and speaking levels of the pupils. Pupils' performance was also examined using alternative assessment and their end-of-year oral assessment. The components assessed in alternative assessment included oral communication. Pupils' artifacts like the digital stories also provided a good platform to gauge the progress of their speaking skill. It was a good way for teachers to assess the use of vocabulary and the ability to synthesise images and ideas appropriately. It was observed that more than half of Tamil pupils were not confident to speak or were not fluent in the language. About 25% of the Tamil language pupils were not able to read fluently.

Teachers' Reflection Notes and Observations

Teachers' observations were recorded in their journals. The entries included anecdotes and reflections. Observation includes noting pupils' engagement level in the lessons and activities.

The indicators for engagement were:

(1) 85-100% active participation in group discussions hands-on activities;

(2) the number of times students edit or re-record their digital stories;

(3) the number of times students contributes an idea;

(4) the number of times students ask each other or teacher to clarify their doubts;

(5) the participation by students who were less responsive (quiet and shy pupils).

Pupils' and Parents' Surveys and Interview

Teachers conducted a survey to find the language spoken at home. This survey facilitated in understanding the home background and the comfort level of usage of Tamil at home. About more than 60% of the Tamil Language students spoke in Tamil respectively, yet they could not articulate fluently at the first diagnostic test.

A pupil survey was also carried out to better understand pupils' interest and motivation of the lessons and activities. Pupils wrote their feedback on the activities they enjoyed best throughout the year. Pupils were also interviewed and parents given a survey on the impact of these activities on the pupils' oral skills.

Discussions of Findings

Authentic Activities

A series of authentic activities with real-world relevance, requiring pupils to examine them from a variety of perspectives, and with opportunities for collaboration were carried out. Pupils were brought to the Jacob Ballas Children's Garden (Singapore Botanical Gardens) to make comparison between their neighbourhood playgrounds with the garden which instill a care for nature. They used Photo Story 3 for Windows to create their own digital stories.

Pupils had hands on experience making murukku, learning the Malay martial arts, Silat. The projects also required them to collaborate and work together. Although the end products may be done individually, but the accumulation of resources (*e.g.,* digital images, vocabulary, peer editing) were done as a group.

Pupils' Engagement and Behaviour

The engagement level of pupils was notably high during the lesson activities was observed. Pupils were also observed to be more persistent as they recorded their readings many times trying to perfect their end products. The peer evaluation process also provided the avenue for them to think through more deeply with their productions. Pupils were actively explored different ways to present their digital stories with technologies (*e.g.,* the Tablet PC, presentation software, sound recording software). Pupils interacted in their Mother Tongue languages more frequently during their Mother Tongue classes. The self construction of the digital artifacts encouraged pupils to take more ownership of their learning.

In addition, the number of tasks completed within the time given also increased. This was possibly due to the pervasiveness use of ICT tools to augment the learning of the languages. The skills acquired from one digital story to another also taught them to use one tool and adapt it into another context. The programme also realized that students learnt to work together. It was observed that they are more engaged when they work in groups. It was noted that the checklist and observations of each pupil gave them opportunity to value students' little progress. Shy students came out of their shell before the year end.

Learning Abilities

In order to bridge the different language abilities and needs, some groups were given additional time to complete the tasks and additional scaffolding. The tasks were tailored to meet average and lower ability students.

Feedback from Parents

According to the parents' survey, the frequencies of the two Mother Tongue languages being used at home increased. A parent reflected the following, "... We are using Tamil more often at home now as compared to before." Some parents reflected that they had been corrected by their children when they did not use Tamil correctly. A parent also reflected that her child had corrected the way she should pronounce the words in Tamil. The drama, show and tell, and storytelling sessions motivated the pupils to practice their lines at home with the family members. Some parents shared that these practice sessions helped them bond with their children. Pupils' survey showed that the students enjoyed the MT lessons. All the students requested for activities which involved use of more computer based activities in future.

Learning with Technology—Creation of Digital Stories

The process of the creation of digital stories allowed pupils to record their own voices when narrating their own scripts. The creation of digital stories places the technology in the hands of the learner and allowing the pupil to control its use within objectives that were constructed by the teacher. Hence, the creation of digital stories was a possible strategy that supported presentation and writing using ICT.

Presentation and writing require skills like deciding goals, sequencing of ideas, composition of message and editing. Simple applications such as Microsoft Power Point and Photostory 3 were used for the creation. These software titles were easily available and widely used in the school. Digital story creation as an ICT mediated strategy could enrich the classroom learning environment, the curriculum, and student learning experiences by providing an open-ended, creative and motivating productive tool in the classroom (Sadik, 2008). Pupils were observed to be motivated and excited in the use the ICT tools to develop their stories which they can relate to.

The element of play also provided an excellent vehicle for learning. Weininger (1978) emphasizes an inner reality (intellectual and emotional life) and an outer reality (world experiences) and the use of play to accommodate and connect these realities. This was evident in the digital stories created by the pupils. (Please elaborate on this point—very interesting if you can elaborate on this) Pupil leveraged on ICT as an output platform to present each of their learning experience.

The digital stories documented the rich experience they had during the play and revisited them to enhance on their projects. Assessment of the project facilitated the teachers in checking on the language literacy and provided the teachers with the pupils' progress.

Issues and Challenges

As with many strategies to learning the usage of ICT has its limitations and challenges.

Pupil ICT Readiness

The initial phase of introduction to both hardware and software was challenging and time consuming. Thus, getting pupils on task using the computers was challenging. At Primary One, many were not familiar with the computer notebooks, let alone the other software titles and programmes. However, the pervasiveness of ICT mediated lessons soon paid off when pupils become more skilful with each lesson.

At times, the pupils may deviate from the task at hand and focus more on the less important features of the presentation. For instance, Microsoft Power Point is an easy and powerful to use for language learning. However, the choice given may be a disadvantage when students start to use too many fonts on one slide or spend more time on the graphics and transition motions than the language objective.

School Infrastructure and Support

ICT-mediated activities could consume many hours when it was an introduction to a new tool and when technical glitches disrupted the smooth running of the lessons. At times, dealing with network problems due to heavy traffic usage was overwhelming.

Conclusion and Recommendations

This study, though descriptive in nature, had shown that the Tamil pupils have been actively engaged in constructing their own knowledge of the Tamil language with the help of ICT tools *(Jonassen and Carr (2000).* Pupils have acquired basic competency in speaking, constructing simple sentences and communicating their ideas in Tamil language. Pupils who come from predominantly English speaking background shows promises of using the language at home. The authentic tasks enabled bonding between parents and child in completing the tasks effectively. As a future direction more authentic activities be introduced in school and laying the context for pupils to leverage on ICT tools to communicate the ideas.

REFERENCES

1. Allwright, D. & Bailey, K. M. (1991). *Focus on the Language Classroom: An Introduction to Classroom Research for Language Teachers.* New York: Cambridge University Press.

2. Jonassen, D., Howland, J., Marra, R.M. and Crismond, D., (2008). *Meaningful Learning with Technology*, Pearson Prentice Hall, New Jersey, USA.
3. Lim, C.P. (2002). *A Theoretical Framework for the Study of ICT in Schools*: A Proposal.
4. *British Journal of Educational Technology, 33*(4), 415-426.
5. Lim, C.P. & Chai, C.S. (2004). An Activity-Theoretical Approach to Research of ICT Integration in Singapore Schools: Orienting Activities and Learner Autonomy. *Computers and Education,43*(3), 215-236.
6. Yin, R.K. (1994). *Case Study Research: Design and Methods (2nd Edition)*. Thousand Oaks (CA): SAGE Publications.

2

Teaching and Resource Building in Teacher Education

— Dr. Seetha Lakshmi

ABSTRACT

This paper talks about the experience of teaching of Tamil language and learning through IT in pre service course training at the National Institute of Education, Singapore. Teachers are undergoing their training on educational history of Singapore, educational psychology and teaching their first and second curriculum studies with the content subjects and practicum at the pre service training. While they are going to be the teachers of 21st century learners, it is essential to equip themselves with the necessary and relevant professional skills. Ida Fajar Priyanto (2007) stated about the production IT based teaching resources for the development of teachers.

Here, instead of learning students' learning and teachers' teaching approaches, they were taught to use, facilitate with information technology and to produce resources for their students and other students. This kind of resource building providing cognitive, social and emotional constructivism based engagement and focus on a common goal i.e. developing the Tamil students in Singapore. The resources were prepared by the writing lesson but can be customized by the teachers for their teaching of other skills in Tamil class. The resources building was based on task based approach, web-quest approach, group investigation approach and multimodal approach. Although the trainees were encouraged to focus on student based learning package they also provided guidelines for the teachers to use it effectively in their class. Here, developing and equipping young students to be the frequent users of the Autonomous Technology-Assisted Language Learning (ATALL) for their understanding and learning of the second language i.e. Tamil (http://en.wikibooks.org/wiki/Autonomous Technology-Assisted-Language-Learning). This way of learning provided the facilitation to the student while he/she learns on his/her own pace in the mode of student based learning with the communication tools for e.g. Computer, sound based media and the content of their subject. A questionnaire was used to collate the trainees constructive comments as they are told to use their and their peers' resources during their teaching Practicum at various Primary Schools for 10 weeks in this January Semester, 2010.

Introduction

Today, information technology has kept the world under its control and has made us all dance to its tunes. We should not forget one thing here. The man, who invented it, when he runs after it, takes on the role of a parent when he strives for its love and comes under its influences to ensure its growth. How do we bring information technology into the education system, and specifically, into Tamil education? Let's look at some the thoughts on this.

As the usage of information technology is prevalent in English, similar efforts are also expended in Tamil lessons. This is commendable. Nevertheless, many questions arises when we look at research sources based on the extent of a student's involvement on information technology in language learning and usage as well as the extent of information technology usage in classroom conversations. I use computers for my teachers and educators in Tamil lessons, my students carry out these activities weekly and some of that can be listed down. However, it sets one thinking on whether a student converses with a computer, or whether students converse with one another to complete assignments or whether a teacher converses with a student to make learning Tamil enjoyable or encourage a student to continue learning with the computer by telling him that he is doing well. This is because our students are well versed with the computer. Today, a five-year-old child knows how to set up a face book account. The child also knows how to change to a new password if he forgets the old one. He knows how to create his own blog. He knows how to chat online with others. However, with these skills, we cannot claim proudly that our child knows everything. The child should know his cultural, language and national boundaries well and does not cross these limitations with information technology. He should know how to protect his mind and body even when he uses this medium. He should learn how to communicate face-to-face even after conversing with the text messages on the hand phone and computer. He should know how to make a stand with his own identity in an environment with people of multi-nationalities and multi-languages. Knowing all these aspects is important; it will be futile without this knowledge.

It is here in information technology that they say that research in Tamil education has not progressed as much as we have. Although the Tamil teachers encourage the students with their love on the Tamil language and passion on their job and strong beliefs on their students' development, still there are areas to improve. At some time, based on the fluent use of written Tamil during the classroom conversation, a teacher should not mention that his/her students are using Spoken Tamil in a confident manner. After teacher training, teachers need to develop them further to excel in their job and equip themselves with the pedagogical approaches. Later they could go into undertaking studies on their students' learning and teach new things. Yes, we need more research studies in Tamil and need to progress in many areas as they can convey much information for future generations.

Let's compile information on usage on information technology in classrooms: From 1988, NIE has been holding workshops and conferences related to information technology. Today, Tamil teachers are well-versed in both computers and the English language. But, they must also be well-versed in the Tamil language. This is important. Computers can be used to teach conversations in Tamil. These technological talents are necessary in the 21st century. It is good to ponder if we can create a good author with the usage of a computer.

We should not use the Power Point software merely as a tool. We should use it as a thinking guide. Lessons should be designed to suit their ages and tap on their experiences and should also allow for their views to be aired. (Gopinathan S., 2000). He further stated that it appears that we do not spend much attention on language pedagogy that understands students' needs and prepares them for global changes and Singapore's long-term visions. In a bilingual Singapore, many have set out to learn about their culture and identity in a language that they are well-versed in. In Singapore's context, this language turns out to be English. (Gopinathan S., 2000). Here, in our today's Singapore context, a number of computer 21 related issues have been resolved. Today, Tamil language should become easily conversant in the classrooms. Are Tamil teachers using computers in the classrooms?

When we focus on teachers, there are challenges that they face. There are some major ones. They are:

- Lack of time
- Inability to spend time solely on teaching as they have other duties

- The absence of appropriate atmosphere or time to read more books to enhance their teaching standards
- Inability to interact with teachers from other schools during holidays as their personal lives do not allow for such luxuries (65 per cent of Tamil teachers in Singapore are women who spend much time with their families).

If we hope to do something for teachers, we can guide teachers to make our generations intelligent. Because, through education, we should prepare our students to live in the real world. Then, with their knowledge and enriched characters, they should make changes to the world and guide the generations to come. The skills of this 21st century are mandatory for this to be made possible. These are information technological skills, discussion tactics and teamwork. We need to tailor our curriculum plans to nurture, appreciate as well as to think of one issue in many angles at any one time. Here, the NIE's new approach on using PB works and is a boon for many of our Tamil teachers' resource production based hopes.

PB Works

This section highlights various ways of using free, web-based software PB works which allow the users to increase their resources and provide passive permission to other educators to use them with proper acknowledgement and *vice versa*.

PB works is software which allows a community to interact and develop further through net. The following are some of the selected features of PB works:

- It is a online community based collaborative and controlled website
- It allows everybody to take ownership and feel empowered
- It provides recognition and encourages competitiveness

- Helps to develop 21st century survival skills (collaborative, soft skills including IT skills and critical thinking skills)
- It has complete access control
- Easy adaptation
- Encouraging learning in a fun way
- Effective audit trailing which assures the citizens feel more comfortable and copyright
- Can do banking in the copyrighted materials without any fear
- The best part is that my students have taken ownership of their wiki. Their writing has improved because they have the ultimate audience—Victoria C, High School Teacher,"(http://pbworks.com/content/edu+resources)
- Free training
- Sharing feelings and critical comments about the content and new initiatives of trainees.

According to its website source, currently PB works "hosts over 300,000 educational workspaces, and has helped transform teaching and learning for millions of students, parents and teachers. (http://pbworks.com/content/edu+overview)"

There is a sample website on how to use PB works for teaching and learning in a useful way (http://pbworks.com/content/casestudies-academic) and websites on the current use of other educational institutions. http://pbworks.com/content/casestudy-northcolonie

Preparation Process

Currently NIE is celebrating its 60th anniversary and it has made history through these 60 years of development and moving higher with more theory based practice oriented teacher training and research initiatives. Recently, at our NIE, we have produced a collaborative report titled, TE 21 and it shares its six key recommendations on refreshing, updating and strengthening NIE's model of teacher education. This covers the initial Teacher Preparation to all the way up to Leadership Training. In other words, it provides training and equips the future teachers with the expected and relevant 21st century skills and following are the main recommendations:

1. Focus on refreshed values, skills and knowledge as necessary pre-requisites for the 21st century teacher.
2. Define a set of professional benchmarks as a framework for developing teacher competencies.
3. Strengthen the theory-practice nexus through mentorship and reflective teaching, among other things.
4. Extend teachers' pedagogical repertoire of instructional strategies, modelled after best practices, to keep abreast of changing content.
5. Develop a high level of assessment literacy in response to changing pedagogies, so teachers can effectively evaluate student outcomes.
6. Enhance pathways and opportunities for professional development to make teaching a profession of choice. (http://singteach.nie.edu.sg/issue-22-janfeb-2010-/206-growing-a 21stcentury-teaching-force.html)

Based on these 6 recommendations, something has been tried in my Tamil pedagogical modules during the last semester and this semester. For the Diploma in Education year 1 and year 2 trainees (28+15=43), I have used them for their pedagogical development. I have explained about the challenges faced by the Tamil teachers and within a minority community, we discussed about their needs too. One of them is getting or producing suitable resources and uses them effectively in the class. Hence this process in teacher training is very handy and timely.

First year and second year students pursuing a Diploma in education course at the National Institute of education, have been told about the resource building and in 2009 they were provided with the training to use the PB which is a website which creates a controlled website. Here, our officer at the Centre for Information Technology in Education provided the basic training to the student teachers. Based on it they have used it on this calendar year and during January semester. The planning are given here:

Preparation Process Teaching Writing through IT for Dip Ed II Class

Although this process involved two groups of trainees, the active involvement is limited to Dip Ed II trainees. I have taught Use of Tamil in Teaching Module (DLT200) for 12 hours within 6 weeks of time span and the following are the main topics taught :

- How to incorporate Information Technology in the Tamil Classrooms (Primary Level)
- How to develop the 21st century soft skills among the students
- Explanation of the PB Works and the Resource Building Initiative

- Creating IT based self-learning package (2 for Continual assessment and one for the major project)
- Sharing of projects on writing and information technology.

Overall, the Learning skills, psychology, pedagogy, proper usage of computer, usage of multimedia, suitable use of spoken and written language were the important areas to be looked into assessing the self-learning package. Here, the assessment of produced works was done at peer and lecturer level. During the assessment round, they presented their individual and group projects in their classes first. They were told to hold discussions in forum styles at that time.

PB Works in Tamil Resource Bank (Process)

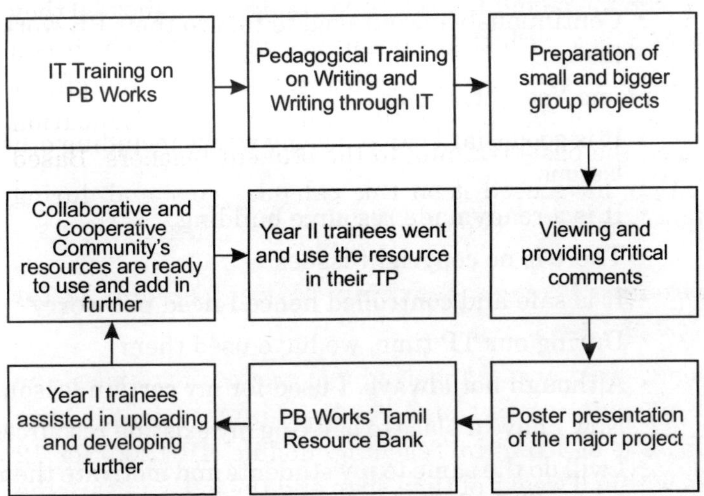

The discussion forum covered areas on which sections were good and why, which sections could be better and why. These improvements were then made and uploaded on the Internet. They created websites with their names and uploaded them. They could then view their classmates' projects as necessary and learn from them. What happened here was that many uploaded projects were done out of their own interests too. This is a commendable initiative. The above picture shows the frame work of the process:

Current Development

Here, currently more than 50 items were uploaded in the PB works website. In uploading the content, the year 1 trainees were very happy to upload their seniors' works with the lecturers' close supervision. In the meantime, they have created their own pages within their folders and started to chat within themselves. They have shared the following comments:

- Very useful
- Motivating them to create more resources and upload
- Indirectly happy to view that their classmates and seniors visited their pages
- Continuously encouraged to talk to their PB works mates

Diploma Year 2 trainees:

- It is good that I can place my works including other lessons
- It is a readymade resource building
- There is no copyright issues
- It is safe and controlled hence I need not worry
- During our TP time, we have used them
- Although not always, I used for my certain lessons
- Now I have a place to banking my existing resources
- I will do the same to my students and motivate them to use IT for learning Tamil in a fun way.

As a professor I feel that this is a good initiative. As there is no copyright issue or no outsider interruption, I am too motivated to parking all my existing projects, power points in this website. For self-centered learning, student based learning, interactive learning, constructive and collaborative learning, this kind of resource building sites are useful and they provide lifelong learning and understanding within their digital natives' community and outside community.

Here, we could witness that many trainees have been placed their personal life related useful sharings and memories. In the sharing on the 'pokkisham', I myself have learned many useful things about my trainees, their intellectual thoughts and of course their heart and mind. It is a learning curve for many others too. I found that these kinds of features are very useful in this process. This PB works have the following key elements:

Constructing Knowledge

Constructivism is building the knowledge the way we see the world. The new experience will become knowledge and scaffolded with the existing knowledge. Through this the human beings are enhancing their understanding the developing their cognitive potential to be an active citizen of his/her community. Here, the trainee teachers themselves construct their knowledge on content, pedagogy and real life related authenticity. At the same time, their future students will also learn the same skills and if possible some new knowledge from this resource.

Interactivity

Interactivity is a feature which is crucial to the success of the social network and it has to be done by proper and planned process. To develop the students as confident speakers and also confident writers, this process will be a good platform and it will be a role model for the Tamil Diaspora outside India and Srilanka.

***Social networking*:** Social networking is vital for making necessary connection between the trainees. The inter and intra social networking enhances the responsibility and the integrity. Here in this project, this is happening and the schools are accepting as the trainee teachers used the products in their Teaching practicum at nearly 28 schools. So, in June another 15 will be trying this pattern of social network and it will become broader and deeper in the following years. As a result, our trainees will create their own PB works for their individual classes and they too invite their all Tamil classes and Tamil teachers to create a social network. At the end, $28 \times 28 \times 6 = 4710$ groups will be spanned and form a bigger network as aalamaram in Tamil. This is a short-term result for us and indeed it will be a bigger and stronger pool for more resources. Yes, this will be a stronger and steady force for many predictable changes in the Tamil students' thought, cognitive, psychological process.

Conclusion

To say that there are no resources is one thing. And to make good use of available resources is another thing. Showing others the usage of the resources and giving permission for this usage is another. At bringing together these aspects is a noble act. By doing this, all our trainee teachers have this facilities in their schools. It is notable that through this, there are many ways they can urge their students to create similar projects and discuss in depth about projects already presented.

REFERENCES

1. Gopinathan, S., 2000. Keynote Address at the Tamil Language Seminar on Teaching Tamil Language in a Fun and Interesting Way. Singapore: *National Institute of Education*.
2. Ida Fajar Priyanto, 2007. Developing IT-based Teaching Materials to Enhance Information Skills and Knowledge Awareness Among Students. *World Library and Information Congress: 73rd IFLA General Conference and Council*. 19-23 August 2007, Durban, South Africa.
3. http://www.ifla.org/iv/ifla73/index.htm
4. http://pbworks.com/content/edu+resources (accessed on 17.04.2010)
5. http://en.wikibooks.org/wiki/Autonomous_Technology-Assisted_Language_Learning. (accessed on 16.02.2010)
6. http://archive.ifla.org/IV/ifla73/papers/133-Priyanto-en.pdf.e-essay. (accessed on 18.04.2010)

7. http://www.clomedia.com/features/2008/December/2464/index.php?pt=a&aid=2464&start=9644 &page=4(accessed on 17 04 2010)
8. http://www.clomedia.com/features/2008/December/2464/index.php?pt=a&aid=2464&start=9644 & page=4(accessed on 17.04.2010).
9. http://pbworks.com/content/edu+overview
10. http://singteach.nie.edu.sg/issue-22-janfeb-2010-/206-growing-a-21st-century-teachingforce. html)(accessed on 17.04.2010)
11. http://pbworks.com/content/casestudies-academic. (accessed on 14.04.2010).
12. Sugiarto Joesoef, 2009. School Leadership Challenges Towards Learning for 21st Century. Keynote Address at the 1st Regional Conference on Educational Leadership and Management on Globalization: *Current Trends in Educational Leadership and Management*. 10-12 November 2009. (unpublished essay).

3

Use of Technology in Running a Tamil School in USA

— Ilango Meyyappan

Introduction

California Tamil Academy's (CTA) primary activity is to teach Tamil to the children and young adults living in America. As an extension to teaching Tamil, CTA also supports developing cultural awareness activities such as music, dance, drama and any art form based on Tamil language and Tamil culture. CTA's mission is to develop a love for learning Tamil that will last a lifetime and develop communication skills in Tamil so that the Tamils in America can appreciate family values and feel the binding with extended family members living in India as well as the US. CTA creates a forum for our youngsters to meet, learn, share and practice our culture and values whereby providing an identity to them. CTA nurtures and preserves our cultural identity and heritage to maintain essential family values and develop self-esteem and pride around the identity by participating in Tamil school and community activities. CTA helps children feel, internalize and be self-assured about the value of Tamil and remove the question of "Why should I learn Tamil?"

CTA Objectives

CTA aims to develop and improve speaking, reading and writing Tamil. Teaching Tamil is much more than just teaching letters and sounds. CTA ensures that the kids achieve small successes every week and that parents are aware of their children's progress in reading, writing and talking in Tamil. CTA ensures that knowledge passes on to successive generations. CTA believes that the kids learn Tamil culture along with the Tamil language. CTA creates a kid friendly environment for students to learn Tamil and has a "Commitment to Excellence" attitude and philosophy in teaching Tamil.

CTA History

CTA was started in 1998 with 13 students. Today, CTA has around 1800 students. CTA was started in Cupertino, California. Now, it is being run in 6 branches in Cupertino, Fremont, San Jose, Folsom, Foster City and Pleasanton. On top of this, CTA has affiliated schools in Novato, Atlanta, Seattle and Phoenix. CTA maintains a student teacher ratio of 8:1. We have around 250 teachers that teach Tamil every Sunday on a purely voluntary basis. With an ever increasing Tamil population in the US, CTA hopes to set an example as a role model school and is sure that Tamils living in other states in the US will eventually follow CTA model, syllabus and curriculum.

Use of Technology

For such a massive operation that is run by volunteers who have other regular full time jobs, the use of technology is very essential in ensuring a smooth operation of the school. We will see how technology is used in the various aspects of running this school and the benefits seen by both the parents and the teacher body by using technology.

User Profiles

Every person that is in some way associated with the school can set up a user profile that has the basic information of

User Role Information	
View	User Role Name
	Admin
	Teacher
	Volunteer
	Parent
	Reg Officer
	Principal
	Attendance Officer
	Book Officer
	TVU Officer
	Treasurer

View My Profile	
User Name	Demo Principal
User Email	ctawebdemo@gmail.com
User Alternate Email	-
Gender	Male
Street	Street
City	City
State	CA - California
Zip/Postal Code	30092
User Home Phone	123-456-7890

the individual like his name, address and contact phone numbers. Each person is assigned a "role" by the management and the system. Based on the "role", each person has certain accessibility restrictions and privilege to a certain kind of information. For example, a parent has only a "parent" role that limits access only to information regarding his or her own child and not any other child. A "teacher" role provides access only to that particular class and not any other class. A "principal" role provides access to all students, teachers, classes and reports only for that particular branch and no other branch. This ensures privacy of personal information and data.

School Profile

CTA uses the regular public schools, private schools and college campuses in the US for classrooms. To create a school like atmosphere and bring seriousness into teaching and learning Tamil, CTA uses regular schools by renting them for 4 hours every Sunday morning. Information about the school like its name, address and location are stored in the system. The classrooms that are being used and the grades and sections for which these rooms are assigned are also stored in the system. The teacher information is also stored. This is so that management is aware of the school and the classes that are being run in each of these rooms.

Student Registration

CTA stopped accepting manual registration using a printed application form and switched to paperless and online registration. From 2009 onwards, all registrations were done online and the payments were also made online. When a student is registered, important information about him is stored in our system and management can access it anytime to contact a student. The school has all the emergency contact information about all registered students so that the student can be helped in case of an emergency.

View Payment Details				
School/Site	Grade	Section	Student Name	This Payment
Fremont	Grade VI	A	[illegible]	200.00
			Total Amount ($)	200.00

Payment Date	9/9/2005
Payment Mode	Credit Card
Bank Name	-
Check No	-
Amount	200 $

View Student Details for :: Shrijan			
Student ID	2083	School Site	Demo School
First Name	Shrijan	Last Name	Swaminathan
Grade	Preschool 1	Section	A
Gender	Male	Date of Birth	10/18/2000
Birth Place	San Jose, CA	Father Name	Swaminathan Krishnamoorthy
Mother Name	Madhu Swaminathan	Street	582 Deerpoint Ter
City	Fremont	State	CA - California
Zip/Postal Code	94536	Home Phone Number	510-796-8313
Mobile Number 1	408-341-5215	Mobile Number 2	408-341-5216
Parent Email ID	swaminathan_k@hotmail.com		
Doctor Name	Dr. Sujatha Tipirneni	Doctor Phone Number	510-496-1222
Dental Name	Precious Dental Care	Dental Phone Number	510-796-7906
EC1 Name	Vijay Doraiswamy	EC2 Name	Subramanyan Krishnamoorthy
EC1 Relation	Uncle	EC2 Relation	Uncle
EC1 Street	537 Amberfield ter	EC2 Street	1890 Hilda Ave
EC1 City	fremont	EC2 City	Mountain View

Student Performance

Teachers maintain an online logbook to monitor and track the performance of the students on a weekly basis. Attendance, classroom participation, reading skills, homework submission are all assessed on a weekly basis and marks for those are entered in the online logbook every week. Monthly test scores are entered every month. At the end of a particular term and at the end of a school year, a report card is automatically generated. The teacher can publish a report card at the end of every term so that the parents can know what scores their children have earned.

LogBook Information

Student Name	Working Date	Homework	Reading / Conversation	Participation
Adithya Kumar	01/17/10	10.0	10.0	10.0
Arvind Kandasamy	01/17/10	10.0	10.0	10.0
Deiva Dharn	01/17/10	10.0	10.0	10.0
Kirthi Ravi	01/17/10	10.0	10.0	10.0
Keerthana Narayanan	01/17/10	10.0	10.0	10.0
Sanjana Murthy	01/17/10	10.0	10.0	10.0
SATHYAPRIYA SARAVANAN	01/17/10	10.0	10.0	10.0
Shreyas Srinivasan	01/17/10	10.0	10.0	10.0
Siddharth Raju	01/17/10	10.0	10.0	10.0

Attendance Details for School : 'Fremont' Grade : 'Grade IV' Section : 'A' Date : '01/17/2010'

Grade	Section	Student Name	Status
Grade IV	A	AdithyaJayachandran	P
		DhanyaDuraivelu	P
		Kathirllango	P
		KrystokaranGanesan	P
		ManishaRavindar	P
		NehaVeerabose	P
		NivethaSivaprakasam	P
		VidyalakshmiMohanraj	P
		VijayRaveendran	P

No of Record(s) :9

California Tamil Academy

Student Progress Report Card for Academic Year 2009 - 2010

School: ' Fremont ' Teacher Name: ' Ganesh Lakshmanan ' Grade: ' Basic III ' Section: ' A

Term	Student Name	Attendance	Home Work	Reading / Conversation	Participation	Monthly Test	Total	Grade
I	Adithya Kumar	9.09	10.00	5.00	5.00	68.25	97.34	A
I	Arvind Kandasamy	10.00	10.00	5.00	5.00	68.25	98.25	A
I	Deiva Dham	10.00	9.09	5.00	5.00	64.75	93.84	A
I	Kirthi Ravi	10.00	10.00	5.00	5.00	66.50	96.50	A
I	Nivethana Narayanan	9.09	9.55	5.00	5.00	66.50	95.14	A
I	Sanjana Murthy	10.00	9.36	5.00	5.00	66.50	95.86	A
I	SATHYAPRIYA SARAVANAN	10.00	10.00	5.00	5.00	66.50	96.50	A
I	Shreyas Srinivasan	9.09	10.00	5.00	5.00	66.50	95.59	A
I	Siddharth Raju	10.00	9.55	5.00	5.00	68.25	97.80	A

Communication

Teachers use web based system for communicating with the parents. The system allows the teachers to selectively choose certain parents or mass email all the parents. Teachers can also post homework details and share documents with the parents. The principal also uses the web based system to send parent and teacher weekly updates that contain information about the school, syllabus, testing schedule, model question papers and make general announcements. The model question papers are uploaded before the monthly tests. The actual question papers are also uploaded and the schools download them and print them out. Since CTA has many branches and affiliated schools, the use of technology is absolutely essential for administering tests.

Multimedia in Syllabus

There is a separate syllabus committee that takes inputs from the teachers, parents, students and other Tamil educators and sets up a syllabus that is tailored to kids growing up in a foreign land where their main form of instruction and learning is in English. CTA uses a lot of multimedia to make learning visual and intuitive for kids growing up in the US. CTA developed and printed its own set of books for reading, writing and exercise for preschool I, II and Basic I, II and III. For grade I to VII, we use the textbooks recognized and used by the government of Tamil Nadu. For almost all grades, we have the textbooks on CDs. We also use other audio and video CDs which have songs, rhymes, poems and pictorial illustrations of letters, words and sentences that make learning easier and interesting.

High School Credit Program

CTA recently got approval for teaching Tamil to high school students towards satisfying the foreign language requirement. With this approval, Tamil students that are in high school can take Tamil as a language and satisfy their foreign language requirement. We use the same system for administering our high school credit program teachers and students. So far, our students have been taking either Spanish or French predominantly for foreign language requirement, now they are happy that they can take their own Mother Tongue and earn credits for that. Only few languages have earned this qualification with the school districts here in the US and Tamil is one of them.

Annual Day

CTA conducts an annual school day at the end of every year. We rent a state of the art auditorium and conduct the events in a professional manner. The entire process of registering for the event, registering kids for the event, uploading of songs and scripts for approval, managing the order and sequence of events are all automated and computerized. Nothing is done manually. We use googlegroups and googledocs to share documents, spreadsheets, create a repository of audio and video files and to automate the approval and registration process. CTA follows strict guidelines to maintain the quality of programs in our annual day. No English words or other language words can be used, no obscene gestures, no vulgar movements and no references to any religion or caste can be used. Only appropriate costumes can be worn by the children.

Annual day is celebrated to add fun to the learning process and also express your cultural awareness in the form of a song, dance or drama. Along with annual day, CTA celebrates Halloween, Deepavali, Thanksgiving, Christmas, Pongal, Tamil New Year and conducts a graduation ceremony at the end of the year. These are all fun related activities that add another dimension to the learning process.

Tamil Virtual University

CTA runs TVU classes right after regular school hours are over. Beginner TVU, intermediate TVU, advanced TVU level classes are offered and many of our regular CTA students take TVU classes and get certified by TVU. We use the same system to register our TVU students, maintain their details and track their performance. Many of our students have been certified by TVU at all levels.

Conclusion

CTA's mission and vision of imparting a high quality and streamlined education to Tamils living in the US is made possible by technology. Tamil education to kids born and raised in a foreign land has its own challenges. We try to solve those problems by putting a process in place that is consistent among various branches spread across the entire country. That process implementation and execution is made possible by technology. As we grow in number, we are also strengthening our technology infrastructure to accommodate the volume transactions and queries. The Internet and web based systems are the future for CTA to effectively and smoothly run such a big organization and operation.

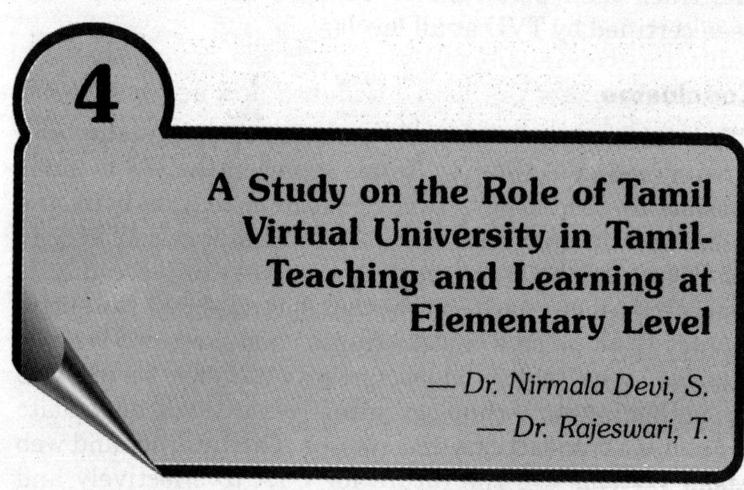

4

A Study on the Role of Tamil Virtual University in Tamil-Teaching and Learning at Elementary Level

— *Dr. Nirmala Devi, S.*
— *Dr. Rajeswari, T.*

Introduction

Education is a process of human enlightenment and empowerment for the achievement of a better and higher quality of life. Education develops the total personality of an individual. It also contribute to the growth and development of the society. The field of education is expanding each year as advancement is made in technology and brain based research.

Technology and Education

New developments and new technologies came into existence and any growing nation cannot remain away from the needs to change in time so that the society is not labelled as under developed and backward society. The process of education cannot ignore the social and psychological impacts of the technology that structures information.

Importance of Teachers

Teacher is a significant agent in causing learning and intellectual development of the learner. It is necessary that teachers keep themselves abreast of new developments. Educators continually strive to maximize the effectiveness and efficiency of teachers by identifying and comparing alternative method of teaching and learning.

Changing Role of the Teacher

During the era of Information Technology the teacher can be called as a mentor, monitor and motivator *i.e.* to develop better learning styles and information seeking behaviour among children. Hence during the 21st century teacher's new role is that of a facilitator and designer of learning experiences and to maintain innovations in the classroom.

Need for the Study

The course of Tamil Virtual University is available free of cost. Any new technology comes not merely with hardware and software but with a learning and teaching style and grammar of its own, and that management practices need to be adapted in order to use the technologies effectively. With poor access and high digital divide teachers tend to resist adoption of e-learning.

To develop teacher competencies in use of web technologies, to plan for capacity building and Training, the teacher's awareness about the functioning of TamilVirtual University, its various teaching modules, their attitude towards the usage of web based technology need to be assessed. This will help the planners and administrators of education to plan and implement in service program to teachers and to make certain changes in curriculum, to make recommendations to the govt the need for improving the infrastructure facilities and technical support in schools.

Need for Technology

Web based learning is an essential tool for achieving sustainability and will help in enabling better and increased access to information to enrich the teaching-learning process.

Tamil Virtual University

The Tamil Virtual University was established in 2000 by the Government of Tamilnadu, aims at providing Internet based resources using multimedia and opportunities for the Tamil communities living in different parts of globe as well as others interested in learning Tamil and acquiring knowledge of the history, art, literature and culture of the Tamil. This is the first virtual university in India for language (Tamil) teaching. Similarly the Indira Gandhi National Open University (IGNOU) started virtual campus initiatives (1999), Netvarsity (1996) first online learning facility by NIIT, Yashwantrao Chavan Maharastra Open University are some of the other virtual universities offering courses through on line mode. Newport Asia Pacific University (NAPU) a new virtual university that offers programmes to teach Japanese as a second language. Nunnan, David (2002). The TVU web based course is designed and given in four levels *viz.*

- Pre Primary Level
- Basic Level
- Certificate Intermediate Level
- Certificate Advanced Level.

The course material is also available in CD. The certificate course is recognized by the government of Tamilnadu. The content given in the CD includes an introduction, lessons related to listening, reading skills, introduction of grammar components, and related exercises, follow up activities, self-evaluation.

Objectives of the Study

- The main objective of the present study is to find out.
- How effectively this web resource is utilized for Tamil teaching-learning processes at the elementary level by the Tamil teachers.
- Which part and which level of the content given in the web is being widely used by the teachers.
- Their attitude towards the usage of this web resource.
- Their willingness to learn the fundamentals of integrating technology in classroom, type of response and interest shown by the students in using web resources.
- Whether students are willing to use this web resources for improving their language skills.
- The encouragement and motivation given to the teachers by the Government and Management, the infrastructural facilities available in the school premises.

Method and Procedure

The present study employed Descriptive Survey research method.

Sample

190 Primary School Tamil Teachers (in and around Chennai and Puducherry) constituted the sample for this study.

Tool

The researchers constructed a questionnaire with 22 statements on a 3 point scale under four dimensions (Yes, No, At times) for this study. (Sample tool is given in Table 4.1)

Analysis of Data

The collected data is quantified and the findings are given as percentage for the responses related to the option—Yes.

Findings of the Study

78% of the sample were aware of the establishment and functioning of TVU, 69% were familiar with the web site address. 60% have expressed that they made attempts to know about the content developed by TVU. 66% agreed that the visual given for writing practice is very useful. 89% confirmed that their students are interested to learn Tamil through the web using Multimedia technology. 86% stated that learning Tamil through this virtual mode is very useful for the students. 77% were of the opinion that this virtual mode has made teaching and learning of Tamil easy. 75% agreed that lessons given at the intermediate level do develop language skills of the students. Only 50% of the sample have stated that they have the relevant facilities in schools to utilize this web resources, 50% thought of using web based technology. 53%, 66%, 77% have agreed for the statement 16, 17, &18 respectively. 77% confirmed that poetry lessons were very interesting. 90% accepted the need for change in the teaching methodology. 61% were of the opinion that there are differences between traditional methods and web based multimedia technology. 84% are willing to undergo training in web based teaching methodology. 90% wanted training in all aspects to use this web based technology for teaching learning purposes.

Educational Implications of the Study

1. Intensive basic training programme, periodical refresher courses must be planned and implemented.
2. The web based learning material CD can be given to all schools.
3. Technology based language teaching to be introduced in the primary level school curriculum.

Conclusion

Since 90% of sample studied want change in the teaching methodology and 89% students are interested in learning through this method if proper facilities and support services along with effective training are provided Tamil that will get a new face in the 21st century.

Percentage Opinion

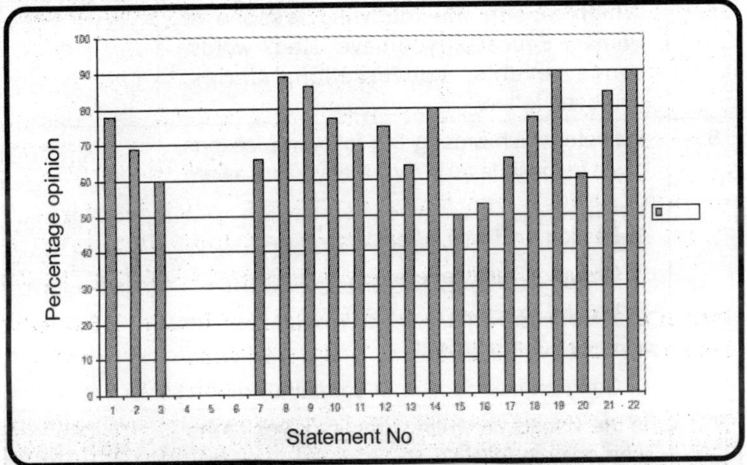

Table 4.1

Sl. No.	Description	Yes/No/ At times
1	2	3
1.	Are you aware that the Tamil Virtual University established by the Government of Tamilnadu has been functioning?	
2.	Have you come across the website of Tamil Virtual University: www.tru.org	
3.	Have you made any attempt to know that the TVU has prepared lessons for school students?	
4.	As of now teaching is done in 4 stages in TVU. Mark the stage which you were aware of 1. Primary Education Level 2. Basic Level	

1	2	3
	3. Certificate Intermediate Level 4. Certificate Advanced Level	
5.	Which among the following lessons of Primary Education you have used? words, songs, events, conversation, stories, numbers, letters	
6.	Indicate which among the following lessons given for basic level in TVU that you are aware of 1. Lesson on Tamil letters 2. Group of Tamil letters 3. Writing Practice 4. Kirantha Eluthukkal 5. Song on introduction of yureluthukkal	
7.	Is the visuals on writing practice given in the web easy to follow?	
8.	Whether students are interested to learn lessons through this audio visual mode?	
9.	Is teaching through AV Mode is beneficial to the students?	
10.	Is teaching through AV mode make the process of teaching easier?	
11.	Whether students are interested to learn through multimedia?	
12.	Is the lessons meant for intermediate level enhances the language skills of the students?	
13.	Do the illustrations given for vatrumai urubu make the students to learn grammar with interest and willingness?	
14.	Are the students willing to learn through the web?	
15.	(i) Do you have any idea of teaching through web to improve the language skills of your students?	

1	2	3
	(ii) Do you have the facility to utilise web for improving the language skills of your students in your school?	
16.	Do you consider the lessons of higher level in the web are equivalent to VI study of formal school level?	
17.	Is the method of practice given in the higher level is easy to learn?	
18.	Is the poetry lessons given in the web motivate learning?	
19.	Do you agree that the teaching-learning methods to be changed according to the changing time?	
20.	Is there any difference between the traditional and multimedia methods of teching in enhancing the language skills of students?	
21.	Are you interested in undergoing training programmes to use web based teaching methods in your class?	
22.	What sort of training you require?	

REFERENCES

1. Anantha Sayanam. *et al. Multimedia as an Alternative Strategy in Teaching-Learning Process in Higher Education*. The Educational Review. Dec.1998.
2. Arulsamy.S (2010). *Educational Innovations and Management*. Neelkamal Publications. Hyderabad.
3. ERIC WEB Sources.
4. *New Trends in Pedagogical Techniques*. M.Phil Education Tamilnadu Open University, School of Education.
5. Panday.K.P. E-learning: Concept, Potential and Future. *Indian Journal of Teacher Education*. Anweshika. 5(1), June 2008. NCTE, New Delhi.

5

ICT for Tamil Education in Tamilnadu Current Challenges and Opportunities

— Prof S.Balaji

Introduction

Tamil is a Dravidian language spoken predominantly by Tamil people of the Indian subcontinent. It has official status in the Indian state of Tamilnadu and in the Indian Union Territory of Puducherry. Tamil is also an official language of Sri Lanka and Singapore. It is one of the twenty-two scheduled languages of India and the first Indian language to be declared as a classical language by the government of India in 2004. Tamil is also spoken by significant minorities in Malaysia, Mauritius and Réunion as well as emigrant communities around the world. The use of technology for Tamil education for students is very minimal. This is due to lack of confidence, demand for the use of English in the application of technology. Eventhough the students appreciate the application of technology in learning and teaching of language, these two reasons prevent them from active application of technology.

Driving Forces

Considering the fact that English is becoming the dominant home language in most Indian households, there is a need to do more to help children from households who have little exposure to Tamil. Therefore, there is a need to review how we teach Tamil, especially at the primary level, so that our students do not lose interest in the language. In particular, teachers need to concentrate on teaching oral communication skills to the younger generation so that they can communicate in the language more confidently, effectively and in greater depth, and will be motivated to use Tamil within and outside of school. Our children have grown up very comfortable with technology—they use mobiles phones, play computer games and surf the net—we should tap on their IT literacy as well as the excellent infrastructure in schools to teach the languages. The illiterate, the physically challenged and the facility-challenged, all of them need some support or the other to be accepted in society and enjoy the fruits. The traditional methods and practices are invariably driven by us, human beings, and therefore tend to be biased.

The introduction of computer (also known as ICT or IT) has changed the scenario to that of an interactive, collaborative environment where the quest for information knowledge is created actively by students. It is here that ICT can help by providing independence, flexibility and variety to the "less privileged learner". This is yet another virgin field, where ICT could have a lasting impact, in terms of enhancing the teaching and learning capabilities, respectively, of the agents of change (teachers) and the beneficiaries (the students).

Impact of ICT

Computer-aided education was initially introduced in India as an innovative activity under the District Primary Education Programme (DPEP) in 1994. ICT entered the education sector through DPEP, which spearheaded the design of school information systems. Literature on the role and efficacy of ICT in education is replete with insightful studies. Resnick (2002) opined that computer was akin to fingerpainting.

In the realm of learning, technology could be employed by students for "making" things, *i.e.,* usage of technology to design and build things of importance. This would consequently increase the acceptance and adoption of technology in the classrooms. Kshetrimayum (2007) elaborated on multiple perspectives germane to incorporation of ICT in teaching and learning processes: simulation, visualization and modelling constituted the pedagogical perspective; assessment forms cognition perspective; e-learning and virtual learning environments comprise content delivery perspective; and finally, from project work and task perspective ICT with a combination of pedagogy & software design could lead to a collaborative environment.

Challenges Ahead

The Human Resource Development Department along with the Department of Information Technology has developed a report on technology in education. The report has identified four issues in integrating technology in education in government schools, namely, ICT infrastructure, quality content that is locally relevant, teachers training, and education delivery through public-private partnerships.These four interdependent issues needs to be addressed if technology has to be integrated to formal education to improve the quality of education in government schools.

A typical rural school has a number of inherent limitations *viz.*, limited number of qualified teachers, archaic classrooms, chalk-and-talk methodology, variations in curricula (state to state and board to board), unreliable power supply and lack of interactions with the rest of the world. The advent of cyber cafes and CD-based courseware has opened up possibilities of alleviating the problem. But, the problem still persists *i.e.,* the non-availability of curriculum- and language-specific material backed up by suitably-trained teachers.

The Pathway for Opportunities

The activities use simple and use commonly available software such as Microsoft PowerPoint. They also provide sufficient flexibility for teachers to modify them according to their objectives, class or pupils' abilities. Much consideration went in the designing of the software such that each lesson constitutes of only a few slides. It was essential that the pupils are not intimidated by the software and hence simple navigation tools were used.We decided against using more advanced authoring software like Mediator, Macromedia Flash or Multimedia Builder as we want Tamil language teachers to modify and enhance our models.

Basic Requirements in using our Microsoft PowerPoint models:

(1) Pupils have

- basic IT knowledge
- basic knowledge of Microsoft PowerPoint
- Usage of recording and playback features in PowerPoint
- Typing text and annotating in different colours and sizes.

(2) Teachers have

- comfortable knowledge in PowerPoint
- using PowerPoint as an effective tool to translate their language teaching strategies into using IT.

The design and use of the software took into consideration the following:

(1) Prior IT knowledge of pupils.
(2) Time needed to complete the lesson.
(3) IT equipment generally found in Singapore schools.

(4) Various skills required for the teacher to design the software.

Human Factors experts have researched the strengths and limitations of different types of the physically challenged and come out with norms and standards for equipment design and HCI interfaces. Experts and researchers have exploited the following methods to make the physically challenged as independent as possible:

(a) Audio cues to help the blind.

(b) Rich graphics to help the deaf.

(c) Combination of the visual and audio cues to help the partially deaf/blind.

(d) Flexible input and output devices for the users with limited movements of the limbs and the body.

(e) A variety of cues to keep up the interest and excitement in children with learning disabilities.

After the stage of memorization and teaching through class representative or leader, blackboard and chalk pieces came about. After which, teaching tools; such as keyboard, computer, smart board, and Tablet PC that consist of computer and mobile phone provide students with the language benefits in class. Tamil letters, Tamil songs, Tamil vegetables, Grandmother stories, are all being sold in the form of CDs/DVDs even in today's commercialized level, and all these have; Tamil's nuances, the beauty of pronouncing in Tamil, vocabulary building in Tamil, India's nature as well as the beautiful Tamil spoken by qualified hosts in their native language that provides a feast for students who hear and view them. Here, the beauty of the language and the benefits of its nativity are displayed in a manner that students can know about. In this stage, we shall see how information technology is used in teaching and learning, at National Institute of Education that trains teachers, who teach Tamil.

Scrimshaw (2004) also points out that the implementation of ICT in the classroom is "both an innovation in technology and teaching" (p.9). On the other hand, multimedia is a combination features of text, graphic, art, sound, animation and video elements with facilities for interaction. Thus, multimedia is a powerful presentation tool, which can be effectively used for teaching. Studies showed that if students are stimulated with audio, they will have about 20% retention rate, audio-visual is up to 30% and in interactive multimedia presentation, the retention rate is up to 60% (Vaughan, 1997; p.10). Hence, multimedia tools can enhance many skills such as, functional communication as a result of enriched vocabulary, critical and creative thinking.

Government Initiatives and Pathway

A need to develop IT Tools to facilitate human-machine interaction, and to promote the use of these tools for various Indian Languages was felt. Towards this, the Department of Electronics of Government of India had initiated activities in the area of Technology Development for Indian Languages with the following objectives:

- To develop information processing tools to facilitate human machine interaction, information processing in Indian languages and development of multi lingual knowledge systems.
- To promote the use of information processing tools for language studies and research.
- To support R&D efforts in the area of information processing in Indian languages covering machine translation, human machine interaction, language learning and natural language processing.

"ICT@school" was one of the important central government schemes formulated in the Tenth Five-year Plan. Its objective was: "promoting usage of ICT in government and government aided schools (particularly in rural areas) and providing ICT infrastructure." This scheme had four components (GOI, 2007a):

1. Partnership with state governments and union territories for providing computer education and computer-aided education to government and government aided schools.
2. Establishment of SMART schools—which will be technology demonstrators.
3. Universalization of computer literacy through Kendriya Vidyalayas and Navodaya Vidyalayas and neighbouring schools.
4. State Institutes of Educational Training to provided educational content in the form of films, videos and audios etc.

The National Mission for Education through ICT has been envisaged as a federally sponsored scheme to leverage ICT so as to democratize education by providing high quality personalized and interactive knowledge modules over the internet/intranet for all the learners in the higher education institutions.

While the Eleventh Five-year Plan (2007-12) has taken into cognizance the importance of education in nation-building, it provided the much needed fillip for expanding the scope of ICT usage in Indian schools. A substantial budget has been allocated towards upgrading technology infrastructure (including ICT) in schools. Targets have been established for reaching out to Upper Primary Schools to have coverage of ICT by 2011-12.

The ICTACT (ICT Academy of Tamilnadu), a consortium of the Centre, State and Confederation of Indian Industry, will provide industry relevant training programmes in the ICT spectrum to the faculty members of the university and its affiliated colleges. Various training programmes will be sponsored by the ICT industry.

End Notes

ICT can help bridge the rural-urban divide, as has been demonstrated by projects that have been successfully rolled out across the globe. Most teachers do utilise programmes such as PowerPoint but only as a presentation facility in their IT classes (as a cognitive tool). Apart from this, commercially available software including e-learning platforms, emphasis lies in self-paced learning. Hence, by using IT as an effective tool to develop the metacognitive skills, we hope to improve their oral and aural performance of Tamil Language pupils.

REFERENCES

1. a b c Gordon, Raymond G., Jr. (ed.), 2005. *Ethnologue: Languages of the World, Fifteenth Edition*. Dallas, Tex.: SIL International.
2. Zvelebil 1992, p. 12: "...the Most Acceptable Periodisation which has so far been Suggested for the Development of Tamil Writing seems to me to be that of A Chidambaranatha Chettiar (1907–1967): 1. Sangam literature – 200BC to AD 200; 2. Post Sangam literature – AD 200 – AD 600; 3. Early Medieval Literature – AD 600 to AD 1200; 4. Later Medieval Literature – AD 1200 to AD 1800; 5. Pre- Modern Literature – AD 1800 to 1900"
3. *Tamil Brahmi script in Egypt*. *The Hindu*. 2007-11-21. http://www.hinduonnet.com/ 2007/11/21/stories/2007112158412400.htm. Retrieved 2008-11-11.
4. *India 2001: A Reference Annual 2001*. Compiled and Edited by Research, Reference and Training Division, Publications Division, New Delhi: Government of India, Ministry of Information and Broadcasting.
5. Seetha Lakshmi and Jarina Peer, (2009). Use of Tamil Language and IT in Tamil Language Education Redesigning Pedagogy International Conference, *National Institute of Education, Singapore*.
6. Sivagouri S. (2001). *Using IT to Improve the Mother Tongue Pupils' Oral Performance by Developing their Metacognitive Skills*—An Action Research. Research Paper presented at the 5th World Tamil Teachers Conference, held at Singapore on Sept 6-8 2001, and Published in the Conference Proceedings. (pp.188-193).

6

Enhancing Activity based Tamil Teaching and Learning using Online Video Repositories: A Data Mining based Approach

— *Dr. K. Vivekanandan*
— *Dr. V. Saravanan*
— *Mr. P. Ranjit*

ABSTRACT

Online Teaching and Learning shows a considerable impact in the education system. The activity based education system introduced by the Government of Tamilnadu in the schools shows a remarkable impact on improving student learning across Tamilnadu. This has been witnessed by many visitors across the world wanting to know about this system and the efforts taken by the Government for successful implementation. The video based interactive tutorial helps the students to effectively learn the contents and also interact with the expert. With the decrease in hardware costs every year, storing much video contents is no longer a costlier process. Data Mining techniques and algorithms are the actual tools that analysts have at their disposal to find similar patterns and correlation in the data.

This paper proposes of presenting the activity based Tamil teaching as short video clips. This video clips are available online to all the students. To start with, set of Tamil teachers are chosen as experts for all the Tamil topics of various classes. The experts' lectures/demo is video recorded and stored in the repository. As the lengthiest lectures will reduce the student interest on the subject, all the lecture topics are divided as short videos and made available for students access. The short video lecture will runs from 3 to 5 minutes. When a student browse through a video lecture and finishes the execution, all the other relevant lectures related to the topic viewed by the students also displayed. The students can easily view the other topics without starting searching for another topics or a topic which cannot be searched very easily. Data mining techniques are used to find the identical patterns. These techniques capture the students' behaviours and also trace through the similar navigations performed by other students across Internet. The related short video contents are grouped together and presented to the students. Grouping of similar patterns are carried out by applying data mining techniques such as Association rule mining (determine implication rules for a subset of video lecture attributes, Classification (assign each video record of a database to one of a predefined set of classes analysis) and Clustering Techniques (find groups of similar video records that are close according to some user defined metrics).

This model enhances the activity based learning and surely will create an interest on "Tamil" or Tamil way teaching among all school/college students. This model can also be used to teach other subjects in all schools/colleges through Tamil. As the telecommunication sector witnesses a major breakthrough using 3G Technologies, all these video lectures can be easily accessed through Mobile phone environment also. The developed model can also be easily implemented by setting up a Multimedia Kiosk/ Centre.

Keywords: *Data Mining, Teaching & Learning*

Introduction

The schools and institutions of higher education have increasingly embraced online education, and the number of students enrolled in distance programmes is rapidly rising in colleges and universities throughout Tamilnadu. In response to these changes in enrollment demands, many schools/colleges/universities have been working on strategic plans to implement online education. The activity based education system introduced by the Government of Tamilnadu in the schools shows a remarkable impact on improving student learning across Tamilnadu. This has been witnessed by many visitors across the world wanting to know about this system and the efforts taken by the Government for successful implementation.

Review of Literature

We began writing this paper with a review of past studies of the issues and trends in online teaching and learning in higher education. A recent survey of higher education in the United States reported that more than 2.35 million students enrolled in online courses in fall 2004 [4]. This report also noted that online education is becoming an important long-term strategy for many postsecondary institutions. Given the rapid growth of online education and its importance for postsecondary institutions, it is imperative that institutions of higher education provide quality online programmes.

Faculty training and support is another critical component of quality online education. Many researchers posit that instructors play a different role from that of traditional classroom instructors when they teach online courses.

Using Short Video for Lecture/Demo

The video based interactive tutorial helps the students to effectively learn the contents and also interact with the expert. With the decrease in hardware costs every year, storing much video contents is no longer a costlier process.

The following are the few advantages for the students by using the proposed approach:

(a) It generates enthusiasm in the students by using interesting or unusual examples.

(b) More useful feedback from students are received by phrasing questions in a positive manner.

(c) It engages the students with leading questions to actively involve them in the classroom.

(d) It encourages collaboration among students.

(e) It gives useful comments on homework.

(f) Simultaneously challenge the students to think and also obtain critical feedback about what the students know by asking the right kinds of questions.

(g) Best to explain specific Tamil topics such as Ilakanam, Seiyul and other advanced topics.

This paper proposes of presenting the activity based Tamil teaching as short video clips. This video clips are available online to all the students. To start with, set of Tamil teachers are chosen as experts for all the Tamil topics of various classes. The experts' lectures/demo is video recorded and stored in the repository. As the lengthiest lectures will reduce the student interest on the subject, all the lecture topics are divided as short videos and made available for students access. The short video lecture will runs from 3 to 5 minutes. When a student browse through a video lecture and finishes the execution, all the other relevant lectures related to the topic viewed by the students also displayed. The students can easily view the other topics without starting searching for another topics or a topic which cannot be searched very easily.

Using Data Mining Techniques to Enhance Teaching and Learning

Data Mining is the technique to explore and analyze the large data sets, in order to discover meaningful patterns and rules. The evaluation of data mining techniques began when the business data are stored in the database and the technologies were generated to allow the user to navigate the data in the real time.

Data mining techniques are used to find the identical patterns. These techniques capture the students' behaviours and also trace through the similar navigations performed by other students across Internet. By considering the proposed objective, this paper proposes the use of data mining techniques to enhance teaching and learning. The major data mining techniques considered in this paper are:

(a) Association Techniques.

(b) Classification Techniques.

(c) Clustering Techniques.

Association: It is method for discovering interesting relations between the variables in the large database. There are different types of algorithm for association rule. They are Apriori algorithm, éclat algorithm, FP-growth algorithm, One-attribute-rule algorithm, Opus search algorithms, and Zero-attribute-rule algorithm.

Grouping of similar patterns are carried out by applying data mining techniques such as Association rule mining (determine implication rules for a subset of video lecture attributes). The students studying a particular video lecture also studies a related content. The associations between the related contents are displayed at the end of a lecture which helps the student to navigate among the interested pages. This increases the students' interest and also creates an indirect interest on the content and learning.

Using association rule algorithms, the subjects associated with other subjects can be sorted out and an impact can be given to the user that; if the user is viewing/studying a particular subject, the association rule algorithms in turn advises to study/view a video that are related to the subject. In this way the related videos are ranked and shown to the user. This will enhance a user to learn more on a subject with all the associated materials related to the subject.

Classification: It is one of the data mining techniques used to predict the group for data instance. Some of the popular classification techniques are decision trees and neural networks. From the existing database, the end user can classify the land with required parameters like state wise, of district wise, area wise and etc. by means of tree like structure.

The above listed classification techniques (assign each video record of a database to one of a predefined set of classes analysis) helps the students to identify a particular subjects and search through specific topics. As the classification process proceeds, the left part or the right part of the tree is considered for better visualization and reading of a subject.

***Clustering*:** It defined as collection of data object that are similar to one another within the same cluster and dissimilar to the objects in the other cluster. Clustering algorithms are broadly classified into hierarchical and partitioning clustering algorithm. Again, the Hierarchical algorithm are Agglomerative and Divisive algorithm and the Partitioning Algorithms are k-means, k-mediod, DBSCAN, CLARA, CLARANS, BIRCH CLIQUE, OPTICS etc.

Clustering Techniques (find groups of similar video records that are close according to some user defined metrics) groups the related subjects and helps the student in choosing related content without wasting much time of choosing what contents to be chosen next or in future.

Discussion and Conclusion

As schools and institutions of higher education continue to embrace and debate Tamil online learning, it is important to envision where the field is headed. It is the appropriate time for us to propose suitable technical model / approached which will help the Government of Tamilnadu to implement the projects better. This model can also be used to teach other subjects in all schools/colleges through Tamil. As the telecommunication sector witnesses a major breakthrough using 3G Technologies, all these video lectures can be easily accessed through Mobile phone environment also. The developed model can also be easily implemented by setting up a Multimedia Kiosk/Centre.

REFERENCES

1. C. J. Bonk, *Online Teaching in an Online World* (Executive Summary), *USDLA Journal,* Vol. 16, No. 1, January 2002, and C. J. Bonk, "Online Training in an Online World" (Executive Summary), *USDLA Journal,* Vol. 16, No. 3, March 2002.
2. C. J. Bonk, *The Perfect E-Storm: Emerging Technologies, Enhanced Pedagogy, Enormous Learner Demand, and Erased Budgets* (London: The Observatory on Borderless Higher Education, 2004); and K.J. Kim, C. J. Bonk, and T. Zeng, *Surveying the Future of Workplace E-Learning: The Rise of Blending, Interactivity, and Authentic Learning,* E-Learn Magazine, June 2005.
3. R. Detweiler, "At Last, We Can Replace the Lecture," *Chronicle of Higher Education*, July 9, 2004, p. B8; and R. Zemsky and W. F. Massy, "Why the E-Learning Boom Went Bust," *Chronicle of Higher Education*, July 9, 2004, p. B6.
4. E. I. Allen and J. Seaman, *Growing by Degrees: Online Education in the United States*, 2005 (Needham, Mass.: The Sloan Consortium, 2005).
5. http://www.educause.edu/EDUCAUSE+Quarterly/EDUCAUSE QuarterlyMagazineVolum/TheFut ureofOnlineTeachingandLe/157426, April 2010.

Open Educational Resources in the Context of Teaching and Learning of Tamil as the First Language

— *Dr. N. Balasubramanian*

Introduction

There has been a paradigm shift in the role of Distance Education universally. Traditionally, distance education was restricted in terms of enrolment because of production, reproduction, and distribution costs. Even though it costs the university in terms of money and time to produce a course, technology has made the reproduction cost almost non-exist which supports the universities in the fulfilment of the promise of right to universal education. At no cost universities could make the content available to millions substantially improving the quality of the life of the learners around the world. The Government of India created its National Knowledge Commission as a high level advisory body to the Prime Minister with an objective of transforming India into a knowledge society. Conceived as a network, the Virtual University for small states of the Commonwealth paved the way for sharing materials and programmes due to the emerging trend of developing OERs which ensures education for all. At this juncture, the present paper aims at discussing how the OERs and other computer and web based technologies could be exploited in teaching a language particularly Tamil as the first language in general and particularly to NRIs of Tamilnadu origin settled elsewhere in the world through Open and Distance Education System.

Open Educational Researches: An Asset for Open and Distance Learning

Open Educational Resources is a relatively new concept which may be seen as a trend towards openness in higher education including movements such as Open Source Software and Open Access. The two important aspects of openness involve free availability in the internet and little restrictions on the use of the resources. The end-user should be free from technical barriers, price barriers and legal barriers on the part of the resources. Besides using the materials, the end user is totally free to adopt, build upon and reuse the same provided the original creator is acknowledged for the work. The participants of a UNESCO Forum in 2002 defined OER as "the open provision of educational resources, enabled by information and communication technologies for consultation, use and adoption by a community of users for non-commercial purposes". It is also defined as "OERs are digitized materials offered freely and openly for educators and self-learners. The use and reuse for teaching, learning and research". The OERs may include (i) Learning Content: full courses, coursework, content modules, learning objects, collections and journals (ii) Tools: software to support the development, use, reuse, and delivery of learning content and (iii) Implementation Resources: intellectual property licenses to promote design and localization of the learning materials.

Mapping OERs

It is to understand that a number of projects and initiatives in the field of OERs is growing fast which include institution based or institution supported initiatives. So far as OER Movements in post-secondary education is concerned, it is found that over 150 universities in China have produced over 450 courses online. The Paris Tech OCW Project formed by universities in France offers 150 courses. The Japanese OCW Alliance formed by nine most prestigious universities in Japan offers over 250 courses in Japanese language and 100 courses in English language. MIT, RICE, Johns Hopkins, Tufts, Carnegie and Utah State Universities in USA have large scale OER programmes. It has been estimated that altogether there are over 2000 university courses freely available online. Australia, Brazil, Canada, Hungary, India, Iran, Ireland, the Netherlands, Portugal, Russia, South Africa, Spain, Thailand, the UK, the USA and Vietnam have already started functioning in the field of OER.

Users and Producers of OER

The typical OER users are to be a single enthusiastic, a well educated self-learner, a faculty member, etc.

The motive in involving OER movements may be that if Universities do not support the open sharing of research results and educational materials, traditional academic values may be marginalized by the market forces. It is also true that free sharing leads to broader and faster dissemination of knowledge which results in development of problem solving skill among the learners besides reducing social inequality. It also increases the popularity, reputation and the pleasure of sharing the resources with fellow users.

Challenges to the Growing OER Movement

Lack of awareness of copyright issues is commonly seen among the users of OERs. Open licensing may ensure controlled sharing with some rights reserved to the author.

However, there has been a growing interest for open licenses which is witnessed by the increasing number of OERs under Creative Commons License. The users of OERs find problems in judging the quality and relevance of such materials. This problem could be managed if the producers use their brand or reputation of their institutions. A review report of the materials prepared by their peers will also help ensure quality. Sustainability of the OER initiatives is also a challenge in the field. Hence, it is important to seriously consider how such initiatives could be sustained in the long run.

Natural Language Processing and Language Learning and Teaching

In learning their Mother Tongue, children develop some remarkable sets of capabilities using which they acquire knowledge and skills enabling them to produce and comprehend an indefinite number of new utterances and judge their properties. Hence, we have to device an explanatory account of the mental operations important for the development of linguistic abilities. At this juncture, it is imperative to seek technological applications to enhance such linguistic skills among learners.

One such technological application is the Natural Language Processing (NLP) supported by computing technology. NLP is concerned with the computational modeling and design and development of a wide variety of systems leading to non-machine communication. The NLP is nothing but the ability on the part of the computer to analyze written text or spoken utterances without limiting to mere recognition of graphics of phonemes but extending even up to the development of an understanding with reference to the task at hand besides integrating various modules with interactive layers. Natural language interface to databases, computers question answering systems, story understanding, machine translations, etc., are some of the applications of NLP which could very well be exploited in teaching a language to children, particularly Tamil as the first language at the international level.

Software for Teaching of Reading & Writing

Lass (1981) identified a number of characteristics that typify good teachers of reading such as ability to organize and manage instruction, attend to individual needs, pace instruction correctly monitoring student attention, monitoring of their achievement, providing one to one instruction when needed and use supplementary materials. Software specially designed for enhancing readiness skills in reading, teaching decoding such as right vocabulary, phonics and structural analysis which include teaching of homonyms and synonyms, teaching of reading comprehension and study skills should be made popular among language teachers for effective accomplishment of language skills among children. Children could be introduced to word processing in order to improve their writing skill. Because of its advantages such as ease of correction, ease of revision, formatting ease, time & effort, quantity and quality of writing, etc. word processing could be the best tool in the hands of the teacher in developing the writing skill among children.

Multimedia and Author ware: Tools for Development of CALL Packages

Multimedia, being a potential tool in the hands of a language teacher, he could develop multimedia packages in different subjects. Even a teacher with little knowledge in computing could do so by using authoring tools such as Author ware, Hyper Cord, Hyper Studio, Mediator, Winwida, Question Mark, etc. Once becoming familiar with the way the authoring tool works, it is then a matter of design rather than programming.

Generally, there are two types of multimedia packages in language teaching, *viz.*, References and CALL Packages.

The References may include encyclopedias and dictionaries. Encyclopedias are the vast collection of hyper-texts, scanned photographs, animations, graphics, human voice, music and video clips. By providing menus and buttons, we can activate the programme and link various parts of it all together. CALL packages help the learner practice the language by providing models of the language in context and encouraging the user to imitate the example in a structured way. Using the record option, an inbuilt facility, the user may record his / her voice and compare it to that of the model and thus the course develop his pronunciate, stress, pausing, phrasing and intonatic.

E-Mail as a Tool for Teaching a Language

E-mail provides a medium for collaborative work using information collected from various locations, besides providing real purposes and audience in relation to the development of literary skills. E-mail helps the teacher introducing, managing and writing up projects due to the facility for sorting all communications. E-mail provides more authentic purposeful exposure to the language in hand and mire meaningful interactive when compared to the conventional classroom activities. This ultimately results in higher level student motivation because of the opportunity given to the learner to practice with the target language in open-ended situations. The writing skill also be improved because of the real purpose with the real people that centres round the activity. Being learner centred and individualized in learning, learners feel free in focusing their areas of interest. Multinational cross cultural discussions, intercultural authropology, review of text, film, etc. may be better e-mail projects for the learners. The phenomenal growth in e-mail use lead to greater internationalization and an increased demand for a world language. It is hoped that by adopting e-mail projects in the context of teaching and learning of Tamil, we can effectively teach the language skills among the learners.

Computerized Question Banks and Online Testing

The computer could be used as an aid to construct as well as administer tests in the context of teaching and learning of any language which enables utilizing the capabilities of the computer system to generate print and administer tests to the learners and score their performances. Networks of computer terminals ensure equally administration of the test directly right to the terminal. Once decoded, the items at the given specifications *viz.*, type of questions, level of cognition, difficulty level and discriminative power, etc., could be printed, duplicated and distributed to the candidates who record their responses on machine-readable forms for scoring. It is possible to call the test items either in the same order as stored or even drawn at random before printing and duplicating. It is also desirable to call the items randomly for each student but printed in different order allowing the students receive a different set of questions.

Implementation process of the testing system involves three natural phases, *viz*,. before the test, during the test and after the test with defined roles both to the teacher and the students in each phase. It is to true that computer technology has come to the rescue of the teacher as well as the students from inhospitable regions of examinations since during testing situation both of them seen anxious. Online testing could also be exploited in the context of teaching and learning of a language since such tests are specially designed for the open and distance learners.

Conclusion

Education is the sector where the international countries have been pumping in enormous funds but still it has not reached the grass roots level of the community. However, it is obvious that everyone in the modern world has a fire to learn and educate oneself which is a healthy indication but offen gets drained due to inadequate facilities. This block could be overcome with the emergence of Distance Education which opened a new window of opportunities to those who wish to accomplish their unfinished dream of acquiring higher education. When this system is supported with technology particularly with increased use of OERs and Computer mediated learning environment, it is easy on the part of the universities to take the Higher Education even at the grass roots level of the community. Hence, it is evident that OERs and other computer mediated language teaching/ learning materials widely available in the web could very well be exploited in the teaching and learning of Tamil as the first language to the aspirants in general and particularly to NRIs of Tamil origin settled elsewhere.

REFERENCES

1. Balasubramanian, N and Kadhiravan, S (1999). *Trends in the development of Computer Mediated Instruction*, Journal of Staff and Educational Development International, 42(2), p.187-183.
2. Creative Commons (2007a). History : "*Some Rights Reserved*" Building a Layer of Reasonable Copyright. Creative Commons. Retrieved November 17, 2007 from: http://wiki.creativecommons.org/History.
3. Downes.S. (2007), *Models for Sustainable Open Educational Resources*. Interdisciplinary Journal of Knowledge and Learning Objects, 3. Retrieved November 26, 2007 from: http://www.ijklo.org/Volume3/IJKLOv3p029-044Downes.pdf.
4. Jan Hylen (2007) "*Open Educational Resources : Opportunities and Challenges*", OECD's Centre for Educational Research and Innovation, Paris, France, from www.oecd.org/edu/ceri
5. MIT (200b7. Profiles : From Diving to Surfing. Retrieved June 7, 2007 from: http://www.ocm.cn/OcwWeb/Global/AboutOCW/Profiles.htm
6. Robert.T Rude (K86), *Teaching Reading using Micro Computers*. New Jersey: Prentice-Hall, Inc.
7. Ronald, M. Kaplan (1980), *Lexical Functional Grammar : A Formal System for Grammatical Representations*. Cambridge: MIT Press.

Computer Aided Learning in Tamil Sentences

— Dr. G. Singaravelu

Introduction

Sentence has unique place in acquiring knowledge of any language and it is a backbone of the language. Learning to make a sentence in Tamil Language is indispensable for better communication. Learning sentence pattern in Tamil is easy but it is difficult to the young learners to acquire the sufficient sentence patterns in Tamil. Present methods of learning Sentences in Tamil are not effective to the young learners in improving their communicative competencies in Tamil. Challenging innovative Computer Aided Learning can be supported to the young learners to learn more sentence patterns for suitable communicative transactions of oral as well as written in Tamil. The researcher endeavoured to prepare a computed aided learning package for acquiring more sentence patterns in Tamil for the young learners at standard IV. . The study enlightens the effectiveness of Computer Aided Learning in Sentences of Tamil at standard IV.

Objectives of the Study

1. To find out the problems of conventional methods in learning sentence pattern in Tamil.
2. To find out the significant difference in achievement mean score between the pre test of control group and the post test of control group.
3. To find out the significant difference in achievement mean score between the pre test of Experimental group and the post test of Experimental group.
4. To find out the impact of Computer Aided Learning in Sentences of Tamil at standard IV.

Hypotheses of the Study

1. Learners of standard IV have problems in learning sentences in Tamil.
2. There is no significant difference in achievement mean score between the pre test of control group and the post test of control group.
3. There is no significant difference in achievement mean score between the pre test of Experimental group and the post test of Experimental group.
4. Computer Aided Learning is more effective than conventional methods in Learning Tamil sentence at standard IV.

Variables

The independent variables namely Computer Aided Learning and the dependent variable namely achievement test score were used in this study.

Delimitations of the Study

The responsibility of the researcher is to see that the study is conducted with maximum care in order to be reliable. However, the following delimitations could not be avoided in the present study 1. The study is confined to 80 students of standard IV studying in Panchayat Union Primary school, Vadavalli, Coimbatore. 2. The study is confined to learning Tamil sentence only.

Methodology

Equivalent group experimental method was adopted in the study. Sample: Eighty pupils of studying in standard IV from Panchayat Union Primary school, Vadavalli, Coimbatore were selected as sample for the study. Forty students were considered as Controlled group and another forty were considered as Experimental group. Tool: Researcher's self-made achievement test was used as a tool for the study. An achievement test was framed for making sentences in different patterns.

Construction of Tool

The investigator's self made Achievement test was used for the pretests and post tests of both control groups and experimental groups. The same question was used for both pre and post tests to evaluate the pupils' skills of sentences framing in Tamil through objective types of question which carried one mark for each question and contained 100 marks.

Pilot Study

In order to ascertain the feasibility of the proposed research and also the adequacy of the proposed tools for the study a pilot study had been undertaken. During the pilot study, the problem under study had been finely tuned. Sufficient number of model question papers were prepared and distributed to 10 students of standard IV in Panchayat Union Primary school, Vadavalli, Coimbatore for the pilot study.

This exercise was repeated twice over two sets of 10 students each. The clarification raised by the students was cleared then and there and the filled answer scripts were collected by the researcher. These students were selected in such a way that they were not part of either the control group or experimental group.

Reliability of the Tool

Reliability had been computed using test-retest method and the calculated value is 0.87. The value is quite significant and implies that the tools adopted were reliable. Hence the reliability was established for the study.

Validity of the Tool

Subject experts and experienced teachers were requested to analyse the tool. Their opinions indicated that the tool had content validity.

Procedure of the Study

1. Identification of the problem by administering pre-test to the both groups.
2. Planning.
3. Preproduction, production and post-production of CAL.
4. Treatment .
5. Administering the post-test.

Data Collection

The researcher administered pre-test to the pupils with the help of a teacher and Headmaster. The question papers were given to the individual learners and evaluated learning obstacles of the learners were identified by the pretest. The causes of low achievement by unsuitable methods were found out. Computer Aided Learning was used in the classroom for learning Tamil sentences for one week. The post-test was administered and the effectiveness of the Computer Aided Learning was assessed.

Data Analysis

Statistical technique test was computed for the study.

Testing of Hypotheses

Hypothesis 1

Pupils of standard IV have obstacles in learning Sentences in Tamil at Panchayat Union Primary school, Vadavalli, Coimbatore.

In the pre-test, Pupils score 23% marks in learning Tamil sentence through conventional method and the Experimental group students score 77% marks. It shows that Pupils of standard IV have problems in learning Sentences in Tamil at Panchayat Union Primary school, Vadavalli, Coimbatore.

Hypothesis 2

There is no significant difference between the pret-test of control group and post-test of control group in achievement mean scores of the pupils in learning Sentences in Tamil at standard IV in Panchayat Union Primary school, Vadavalli, Coimbatore.

Table 8.1

Stages	N	Mean	S.D.	df	t-value	Result
Pre-test control group	40	12.58	2.90	78	0.17	Insignificant at 0.05 level
Post-test control group	40	12.70	3.12			

The Table 8.1 showing achievement mean scores between pre-test of control group and post-test of Control group.

The calculated 't' value is (0.17) less than table value (1.99). Hence null hypothesis is accepted at 0.05 levels. Hence there is no significant difference between the pre-test of control group and post-test of control group in achievement mean scores of the learners in learning sentences in Tamil.

Hypothesis 3

There is no significant difference between the pre-test of Experimental group and post-test of Experimental group in achievement mean scores of the pupils in learning Sentences in Tamil.

Table 8.2

Stages	N	Mean	S.D.	df	t-value	Result
Pre-test Experimental group	40	12.58	2.90	78	0.17	Insignificant at 0.05 level
Post-test Experimental group	40	12.70	3.12			

The table 8.2 showing achievement mean scores between pre-test of Experimental group and post-test of Experimental group.

The calculated 't' value is (8.67) greater than table value (1.99). Hence null hypothesis is rejected at 0.05 level. Hence there is significant difference between the pre-test of Experimental group and post-test experimental group in achievement mean scores of the learners of Tamil sentences.

Hypothesis 4

Computer Aided Learning is more effective than existing methods in learning sentences in Tamil at standard IV.

Achievement mean scores of the learners in post-test of control group is 12.70 and the achievement mean scores of the learners post-test of Experimental group is 19.65. Score of the post-test of Experimental group (19.65) is greater than pre-test of Experimental group (13.70). It shows that learning sentences by using Computer Aided Learning is more effective than conventional methods.

Findings

1. In the pre-test, Pupils score 23% marks in learning Tamil sentences through conventional method and the Experimental group students score 77% marks. It shows that Pupils of standard IV have problems in learning Sentences in Tamil at Panchayat Union Primary school, Vadavalli, Coimbatore.
2. There is no significant difference between the pre-test of control group and post-test control group in achievement mean scores of the pupil of standard IV in learning Tamil sentences through Computer Aided Learning at Panchayat Union Primary school, Vadavalli, Coimbatore.
3. There is significant difference between the pre-test of Experimental group and
4. Post-test of Experimental group in achievement mean scores of the pupils in i-learning Tamil sentences.
5. Computer Aided Learning is more effective than existing methods in learning i-sentences in Tamil at standard IV.

Educational Implications

1. Computer Aided Learning in Tamil can be extended to primary level, secondary level and higher secondary level.
2. It can be encouraged to implement to use in adult education.
3. It may be activated in teachers education.
4. It may be implemented in alternative school.
5. Eliminating the problems of slow learners by using it.
6. It may be more supportive to promote Sarva Siksha Abiyan in grass root level.

Conclusion

The study reveals that students of standard IV in Panchayat Union Primary school, Vadavalli, Coimbatore have problems in learning Tamil sentences through conventional method. Learning sentences in Tamil through Computer Aided Learning is more effective than conventional methods. Hence it will be more supportive to enrich sentences in Tamil at primary education.

REFERENCES

1. Ray, William, S., (1960). *An Introduction of Experimental Design*. The Macmillan Company: New York.
2. Ravichandran.T, *Computer Assisted Language Learning*, (Paper Presented and Published in the Proceedings: National Seminar on CALL, Anna University, Chennai, 10-12 Feb. 2000, pp. 82-89.)
3. Vasu Renganathan, (2009). *Enhancing the Process of Learning Tamil with Synchronised Media*, Tamil Internet Conference, INFITT: Germany.
4. Singaravelu.G, (2009). *Effectiveness of Multimedia Package* in Learning Vocabulary in Tamil. Tamil Internet Conference, INFITT: Germany.
5. Sampath, K., Paneerselvam, A. and Santhanam. S., (1998). *Introduction to Educational Technology*, Sterling Publishers Pvt. Ltd.

9

Moodle: For Enhanced Learning
(Tamil Language)

— Ravishankar Somasundaram

Introduction

As we all know "The Webolution (web-evolution)" has changed the way we live. How many of us still have the fear of getting lost without knowing our way in some foreign region? From household utilities to online traffic monitoring systems the web has its part to play, to mention about the way it has impacted the learning aspects, companies foresee a save on range of millions bringing in the e-learning concept into their environment.

Having worked on the lines of mashing up cutting edge technologies along with learning aspects to provide e-learning solutions, I suggest Moodle – one of the best available in market today to deliver e-learning content.

What do I Gain on Reading Further?

Through this paper you will get to know what an LMS is and why do we need to adopt one for learning Tamil language. We will also see how can it make a difference in today's conventional way of learning and a combination of why moodle is the best choice, what can it offer, what moodle cannot offer and how can we compensate it to bring in maximum learning effectiveness by employing featured customizations based on research on this platform in a way it suits best for teacher and student.

Aiming the applications of this platform in Tamil language teaching, have created a demo course in Tamil language which illustrates in detail the usage of all features (types of resources and activities) which can be utilized within a course to form course content.

The course can be accessed under Tamil category in this site (http://demo.moodle.net/login/index.php); having covered the existing features of moodle by other presenters as well the demo course mentioned above, this paper is primarily going to focus on the featured customizations to enhance the learning.

- **Curriculum Management**

Necessity: To avoid the student turning aimless and cruise within the site as no boundaries/learning objectives has been set for him to progress in achieving his goal.

Features: Creating and maintaining course, module hierarchy, Course completion methodologies and roles associated with the curriculum.

- **Learning Effectiveness**

Necessity: To help, motivate, monitor the student progress along with their peers.

Features: Includes Learning Curve mapping and Statistics which results in a healthy competition with their fellow students on comparing their grades.

What is an LMS?

LMS = Learning Management System, as it name indicates

a software application for managing, administering, documenting and tracking learning content which involves students and teachers with respect to learning objectives. In other words it's a software package which delivers a new and effective methodology of teaching and learning for both students and teachers via network or as a standalone pack.

Why do we need an LMS for learning Tamil Language?

Because a system which can make a global reach is need of this hour, using an LMS we—

- Open up a possibility of working with people who aren't physically with you either sometimes or all of the time.
- Help students who are studying in a typical class room environment this by providing a continuous learning opportunity using which he can not only be in touch with the learning concepts studied in the class but actually enhance it by discussing, clarifying his doubts, answering others doubts and by taking part in other forms of activities with or without the help of resources provided within the LMS.
- Uniting people all over the world in the name of Tamil by providing a channel for communication between people, who are
  - — Experts in Tamil language
  - — Dedicated towards learning Tamil language
  - — Interested to know about Tamil language

Irrespective of their geographical location.

How can it Bring a Difference?

It can have a tremendous impact because of the learning methodology and flexibility it provides to students and facilitators. Have quoted few:

Students

- Provides the flexibility for students to attend the course in their desired timings.
- Students have a reach to the teacher/facilitator even if they are not online.
- Majorly it not only makes students familiar with computer and web portal usage but also inculcates the blended learning approach and community discussion qualities which are a must to have qualities on higher stages of their career.

Teacher/Facilitator

- Accommodate more students than it is possible in a typical class room setup.
- Opens up possibility on conducting events like "Experts corner, Facilitators week . . . etc" which needs dedicated time of a guest sharing real time situations with students which becomes often less possible in a class room setup because of the necessity of guests physical presence amongst their varying busy schedule.
- Single repository to store all course related materials thus preventing deterioration with time, and making them available through ages.

Overall the throughput of students as well as teacher is high due to the flexibility an LMS adds up to their learning environment.

Why Moodle?

Strong user Base

Moodle is established in 206 countries, its count on number of registered sites is 46,995 which give the reliability that the future development of moodle is no way diminishing.

Healthy Support

A software package no matter to what extent it can outperform others in functionality and other aspects, without a manual it is used less/useless. Moodle not only have a vast group of individuals who regularly contribute to documentation and try to keep it up to date, what makes moodle special is the densely populated forums where you get answers for any question from co-moodlers almost immediately.

Open Source

As familiarly known moodles source code is freely available under GPL license, in case of doubts regarding moodle becoming proprietary or getting sold to some X company in future, here (http://docs.moodle.org/en/Future) is a comprehensive material for you.

What can Moodle Offer?

Moodle can offer a perfect teaching and learning environment for both students and teachers along with powerful mechanisms to validate the theoretical as well as implied, applied learning acquired by the students.

What Moodle does not Offer as of Now?

Present version of moodle does not offer the following important features:

Mapping the learning curve attained by the student and formulate a focused attention to required students on required areas.

As a facilitator it is our responsibility to indicate it to the students their strengths and weakness.

For example, Theoretical knowledge and applied knowledge.

We need to measure and show the student whether he is good in applying the concepts learned in the classroom. In many cases we notice that a student has good knowledge on theory but fails to apply on real time situations, hence focus has to be given on that phase for that particular student.

Providing a statistics on what is happening around him in the online class room with respect to learning.

Because the students are getting trained in a VLE (Virtual Learning Environment), they lose the opportunity to have a healthy competition with their fellow students by comparing their grades.

Thereby not knowing their stance in the class, this can diminish the interest within students on learning online on due course of time.

Manage the flow between constituents of a course and between courses themselves to form a curriculum.

To emphasize the necessity and importance of a curriculum management system consider this scenario.

A portal which is dedicated for learning Tamil language, containing different courses starting from basics of Tamil (alphabets) to writing a comprehension. Now a student enters the site with an aim to attain expertise in Tamil, and all he sees is multiple courses, now here the student.

1. Can skip one or multiple mandatory courses knowingly or unknowingly.
2. Can jump resources/activities/courses as a learning structure doesn't restrict him in doing so.
3. Gets lost often when he logs into the site without knowing where he left last time.
4. Might not know when he has to go to next activity or resource/activity/course.

Solution?

Developing a solution with keeping the above issues in mind along with usability factor was challenging.

Curriculum Management

Necessity

To avoid the student turning aimless and cruise within the site as no boundaries/learning objectives has been set for him to progress in achieving his goal.

Add-on

Curriculum functionality was designed, implemented, and was subjected to all kinds of tests; the final product has been contributed in moodles contrib section. You can find it in here (http://tracker.moodle.org/browse/CONTRIB-1604). Presently this functionality is up and running on a site which was built to handle 3000 concurrent users and 20,000 users overall using (Cloud computing - Amazon EC2).

Features

Creating and maintaining courses along with module hierarchy, Course completion methodologies and roles associated with the curriculum.

Course Hierarchy

1. There can be a tree hierarchy
2. There can be a parallel hierarchy
3. There can be a serial hierarchy.

Between courses inside the curriculum, the admin. has the power to tailor the courses in any of above mentioned hierarchies.

Module Hierarchy

1. There can be a tree hierarchy
2. There can be a parallel hierarchy
3. There can be a serial hierarchy.

Inside a course or a curriculum, the admin/teacher has the power to tailor the activity/resource flow in any of above mentioned hierarchies. If a course/curriculum has elements following any of the above mentioned hierarchy, it is said to be possessing dependencies.

Course Completion

Completion of a course for any student occurs on two ways,

Automatic

Any student is marked as he completed the course if he completes the dependencies within the course; once he completes this course automatically he gets access to other courses which are dependent on this course.

Manual

A student takes a course and even though he finished all locks/dependencies he will not be marked as he completed the course until the teacher manually specifies that he/she is qualified enough to move to further. And any student enrolled in a curriculum is enrolled in all the courses within the curriculum but denied access to courses as per the hierarchy structure designed by admin/teacher. Teacher/admin has the facility to suspend the user for any single course or multiple courses in case he violates some rules for that course/curriculum itself.

Roles

1. Curriculum wide (similar to site wide roles)
2. Course wide (similar to course wide)

Learning Effectiveness

Learning Curve Mapping

Necessity

To help, motivate, monitor the student progress along with their peers.

Add-on

This functionality was designed, implemented, and was subjected to all kinds of test's, the final product has been implemented in sites where users from diverse backgrounds and job natures find it impeccably meeting the motto which is to help, motivate, monitor the student progress along with their peers and create a healthy competition between them.

Features

Includes Learning Curve mapping and Statistics which results in a healthy competition with their fellow students on comparing their grades.

Statistics

Indicating the current position of the student amongst his peers using discrete scatter plot.

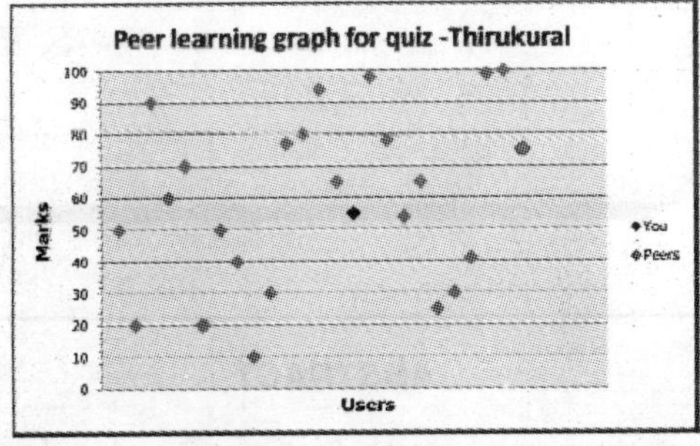

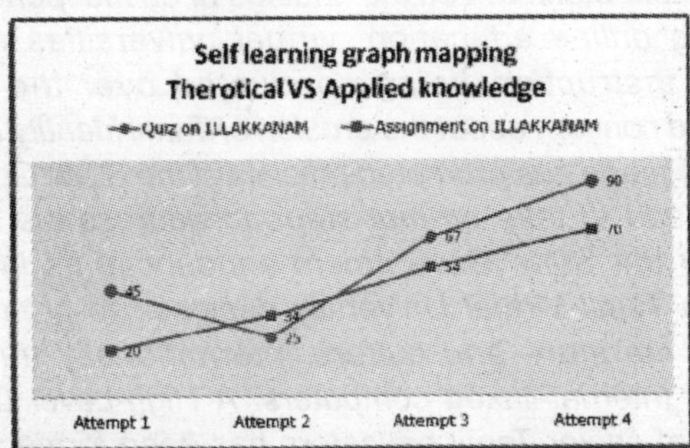

Indicating the learning curve of required activities for a student, quiz mapping to get the learning curve on theoretical knowledge and Assignment mapping to get the learning curve on applied knowledge using continuous line plot.

Quality Analysis of Tamil Virtual University

— *S. Rajkumar*

ABSTRACT

This document summarizes the findings of an independent study concerning online education, virtual universities and Tamil language instruction being conducted over the Internet. Widespread concern about the erosion of Tamil identity and decay of Tamil language has prompted officials of the State Government of Tamil Nadu to take prompt steps to address the issues. In early 1999 the State Government announced its intention to establish a Tamil Virtual University designed to promote Tamil language, literature and culture internationally through the medium of Internet-linked computers. A High-Level Committee consisting of senior Tamil educators has been formed and sub-committees drawn up with a mandate to formulate the vision and mission of the Tamil Virtual University, issue a detailed report to the State Government with recommendations. Thus we are going to analyse what exactly people needs and requirements through a technique called Quality Function Deployment (QFD).

QFD is a methodology for incorporating the Voice of the People (VOP) into the practical design. It aims to capture and prioritise people requirements and translate them into design requirements through the use of management and planning tools such as affinity diagrams, tree (hierarchy) diagrams, relations diagrams, matrices and tables.

QFD can be used to analyse the TVU such as

- How can we extract people requirements and prioritise them?
- How can we identify the key design requirements that will help satisfy our people?
- Which people requirements should we be focusing?
  1. Understanding people Requirements
  2. Quality Systems Thinking + Psychology + Knowledge/Epistemology
  3. Maximizing Positive Quality That Adds Value
  4. Comprehensive Quality System for Satisfaction.

Thus the Tamil Virtual University Encloses

- Understanding 'true' needs from the people perspective
- What 'value' means to the people, from the people perspective
- Understanding how people or end users become interested, choose, and are satisfied
- Analyzing how do we know the needs of the people
- Deciding what features to include
- Determining what level of performance to deliver
- Intelligently linking the needs of the people with design, development, engineering, manufacturing, and service functions
- Intelligently linking Design with the front end Voice of people analysis and the entire design.

The Tamil Virtual University website should include:

- a virtual campus 'map' of programmes and offerings on its home page;
- an attractive TVU logo or banner on each TVU Web page;
- a complete listing of course offerings at Tamil Nadu universities;
- information about admission to institutions of higher learning in Tamil Nadu; and
- A listing of faculty and staff engaged in the TVU project.

Objectives of the Analysis

- To deliver online learning to geographically separate Tamil communities;
- To deliver customized programmes for the promotion of Tamil language and culture;
- To develop educational courses to address the needs of Tamils living abroad.

Mission

1. To develop and deliver Internet based learning material in Tamil language, literature and culture to global Tamil Communities and others interested.

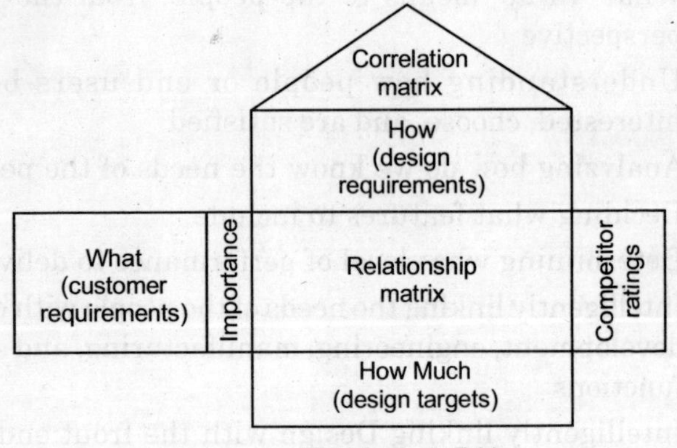

TVU Analysis Table

	Material		Clear to Point	Comfort View		quality	Satisfaction	ServiceAbility	Season Complex	Design Aspects	Look and feel	appearance				volume	convenience	availability	Return visit rate	Targeting	performance	Target value
Audio & video resources	♠		△	♠		●	●	♠	♠	△	△		♠	△		♠		♠		♠	3	4
e-texts	♠	♠			△	♠	●			♠		△				♠		♠		♠	1	4
People feedback			△		●			●			△						△			♠	2	5
helpline					△	♠	●	♠			△				♠		♠	♠		△	2	5
Message board		●	●	△		♠		●	♠			△	△	♠			♠		△	△	1	5
Comment box			♠	●	△		●		△		△			♠			△		♠		2	4
quality	●	●	●	●	♠	●	●	△				△			♠	●		△		●	3	5
hyperlinks	♠	●		♠	♠					♠	♠			△			△	♠			2	4
Glossary			♠	♠			♠	♠		△		△		△			♠			△	2	4
Course pack	♠	♠		♠			♠	♠				●		♠		♠		♠		♠	3	5
Library resources	♠				♠	●		△		△	♠	●	△			♠		♠		♠	3	4
Books collections	♠	♠		△		△	●	♠	△		♠		♠	△		♠		♠	♠		3	4
Essay collection		♠	♠	△		●		●				●	♠			△	♠	♠		●	1	4
Poetry collection	♠	♠		♠	△	♠	♠	△			♠			♠		♠		△		♠	1	4
History details	♠					●	♠	△				●	♠			♠	♠	△		●	1	4
Down loading options						●	♠	△						♠	♠	♠		♠		♠	1	3
Remain interested	♠		♠	♠		●			♠	♠		♠		△			♠	△	△	△	2	5
Casual environment		♠	♠	♠		△	△			♠		♠						●	△	●	2	4
Dates and calendar		△		♠		△		●				●		△				△		♠	1	3
Tvu logo and banners	♠			△	△	△	△		♠	△	♠		●			♠			△	●	2	4
Tvu project details	♠	♠		♠		●	●	△			♠		△			♠		♠		●	3	4
Campus map		♠			△			●		♠	♠				△	♠					3	4
Press releases		♠		♠	△	△	●		△			△		●			△	●		♠	1	3
Recent visited blogs			♠	△		●	△		●					●	●		△		△	●	1	3
performance	4	3	3	3	3	3	2	3	2	3	2	3	2	3	2	2	2	3	2	3		
target	5	4	4	4	4	5	5	4	4	4	4	4	4	4	4	4	4	4	5	5		

2. To initiate and continue necessary measures to co-ordinate and pool together knowledge resources, developed in Tamil in different parts of the world, for wider dissemination.

Steps in QFD in TVU

- Plan collection of people needs.
- Prepare for collection of people needs. Identify required information. Prepare agendas, list of questions, survey forms, focus group/user meeting presentations.
- Determine people needs or requirements. Document these needs. Consider recording any meetings. Extract statements of needs from documents. Summarize surveys and other data. Use techniques such as ranking, rating, paired comparisons, or conjoint analysis to determine importance of people needs.
- Use affinity diagrams to organize people needs. Consolidate similar needs and restate. Organize needs into categories. Breakdown general people needs into more specific needs by probing what is needed. Once needs are summarized, consider whether to get further people feedback on priorities. Undertake meetings, surveys, focus groups, etc. to get people priorities. State people priorities using a 1 to 5 rating. Use ranking techniques and paired comparisons to develop priorities.
- - strong(5) c – medium (3) □– weak(2)

TVU Planning

- Organize people needs in the Product Planning Matrix. Group under logical categories as determined with affinity diagramming.
- Establish critical internal people needs or management control requirements.
- State people priorities. Use a 1 to 5 rating. Critical internal people needs or Develop competitive evaluation

of current TVU. Use surveys, people meetings or focus groups/clinics to obtain feedback. Rate scale with "5" indicating that the TVU fully satisfies the people needs.

- Review the competitive evaluation strengths and weaknesses relative to the people priorities. Determine the improvement goals and the general strategy for responding to each people need. The Improvement Factor is "1" if there are no planned improvements to the competitive evaluation level. Add a factor of .1 for every planned step of improvement in the competitive rating, (*e.g.*, a planned improvement of going from a rating of "2" to "4" would result in an improvement factor of "1.2".
- The process of setting improvement goals and sales points implicitly develops a product strategy. Formally describe that strategy in a narrative form. This strategy brief is typically one page and is used to gain initial focus within the team as well as communicate and gain concurrence from people improvement factor, and the weighting factor associated with the relationship in each box of the matrix.

Conclusion

Thus QFD is a methodology for incorporating the Voice of the People (VOP) helped to develop content that are attractive and suit the needs of young people living in foreign cultures, they will frequent the TVU Website and make use of its course offerings as auditors at first and deliver customized programmes to meet the cultural needs of the Tamil Communities in different parts of the world and help them retain contact with their heritage. So that to facilitate easy access to other online resources already developed by the international Tamil communities.

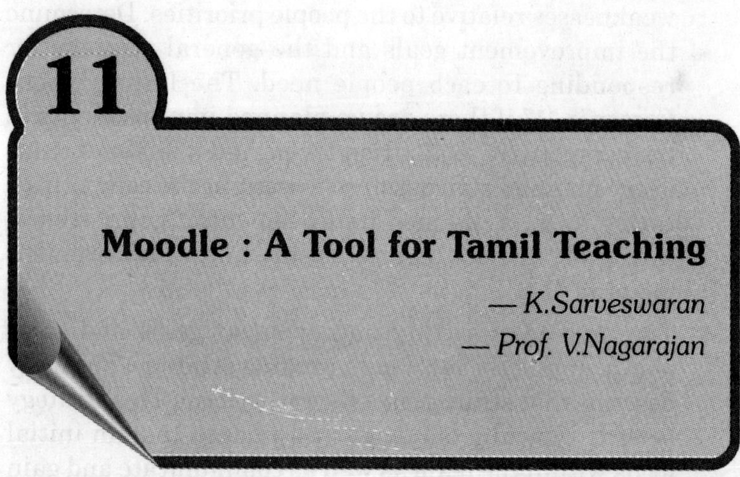

11

Moodle : A Tool for Tamil Teaching

— K.Sarveswaran

— Prof. V.Nagarajan

ABSTRACT

Tamil language teaching has become an important need in the Tamil Diaspora, especially for the young generation. Constructing knowledge through interactions and collaboration is proved as an effect and efficiency method, which is referred as social constructivist learning, especially when the learners have some prior knowledge. The web 2.0 encourages collaboration. The e-Learning 2.0 is proposed based on Web 2.0 and constructivist learning. Moodle is a Free and Open Source Learning Management Software. The Moodle is developed based on E-Learning 2.0. As a result the Moodle provides space for collaborative learning through new cutting edge web 2.0 technologies, which in turn provides for effective learning. The young generation of Tamil society is familiar about Web 2.0. Therefore the Moodle is a good tool for Tamil language teaching.

Introduction

Social Constructivist Learning

Pedagogy refers to strategies of instruction, or a style of instruction [1] that is used to construct knowledge. Teachers use different styles of instructions to construct knowledge based on their experiences. A teacher can not convey knowledge to every student on the same level during a lesson, however implementing a variety of instruction styles in a course allows all the students to learn in at least one way that matches their learning style. Researches have been showing that the best way to learn is by having students construct their own knowledge instead of having someone construct it for them. The instruction style that helps to construct knowledge in this way is called as Constructivist Learning [2]. The prior knowledge of the learners is important and it may help constructing knowledge. The prior knowledge comes from past experiences, culture, and their environment of the learners [2]. Therefore even when teacher constructs new knowledge the prior knowledge of the learners should be considered.

Social constructivist learning extends the constructivism into social setup and it is defined as groups of learners construct knowledge for one another, collaboratively creating a small culture of shared artifacts with shared meanings. When one is immersed within a culture like this, one is learning all the time about how to be a part of that culture, on many levels [3].

The knowledge can be shared in the forms of audio, video, text, 3D animations, question and answer, discussions, etc[2]. The percentages in Table 11.1 represent the average amount of information that is retained through different forms of knowledge [2].

Though these forms can be used to some extent in face—face scenarios, when it comes to remote teaching it was difficult to share these forms of knowledge among learners in the past.

Table 11.1 : Average amount of information retained vs style of instruction

Style of instruction	Average amount of information retained
Lecture	5%
Reading	10%
Audiovisual	20%
Demonstration	30%
Discussion Group	50%
Practice by doing	75%
Teach others/immediate use of learning	90%

Web 2.0

Web 2.0 is the current standard of Web. The earlier web 1.0 was the read only web and the web site authors only could share the knowledge and the people who read could not share the reflections or their knowledge. Web 2.0 introduces many techniques that let authors and readers to share the knowledge.

The techniques are Wiki, Forum, Blog, Chat, Web group. Social networking is also a resultant of all these techniques of Web 2.0.

E-Learning 2.0

e-Learning can be explained as learning that is supported through an electronic medium [4]. Due to the feature and facilities of the web is heavily used for e-Learning. The E-Learning 2.0 is came with the arrival of Web 2.0. The version 2.0 of electronic learning encourages the collaborative learning, constructing knowledge through Web 2.0 technologies such as Wiki, Forum, Mailing groups, social networking, blog etc.

Moodle

Moodle is an Open Source Learning Management Software, which is developed based on E-Learning 2.0 standard and the principles of social constructionist pedagogy. Moodle provides many activities related to collaborative learning such as Wikis, Blogs and Forum to implement this pedagogy. Moreover, the software is currently available in more than 70 languages including Tamil and also been used in more than 200 countries. All around the world there are many courses that are from K12, Undergraduate and Post graduate courses are conducted through Moodle. In Sri Lanka recently the University of Jaffna has started a Online BBM in Tamil medium using Moodle. However Moodle is been used in Sri Lanka for more than 5 years.

Teaching and Learning through Moodle

Moodle facilitates for the traditional teacher-led learning and the new type called social constructivist learning that is discussed in the section 1.1. Also the Moodle can be used as a part of blended learning, where the learning is conducted both face to face and e-Learning modes. The main components of Moodle are resources, Activities and other collaborative features like participants, messaging, calendar etc.

Resources

According to the teacher led methodology the teacher can share their knowledge in form of Microsoft Word and Microsoft PowerPoint, Flash, Video formats, Audio formats and Portable Document Formats (PDFs). More importantly these can be viewed in the Moodle it self without any other supporting tools. In terms of Moodle all these are referred as resources. In addition to these resources, it also lets to create Internal web pages (HTML formatted) using inbuilt HTML editor, Internal text pages and also facilitate to link Files that are stored locally or in remote locations such as web.

Moodle also has a file repository to which we can upload files and can use them. All types of need of learners can be severed by Moodle as it is supporting for many types of contents.

Not only just having resources but also those can be arranged according to the instruction style a teacher would like to follow. The resources can be easily added and edited. Figure 11.1 shows a part of Moodle page where some resources are used.

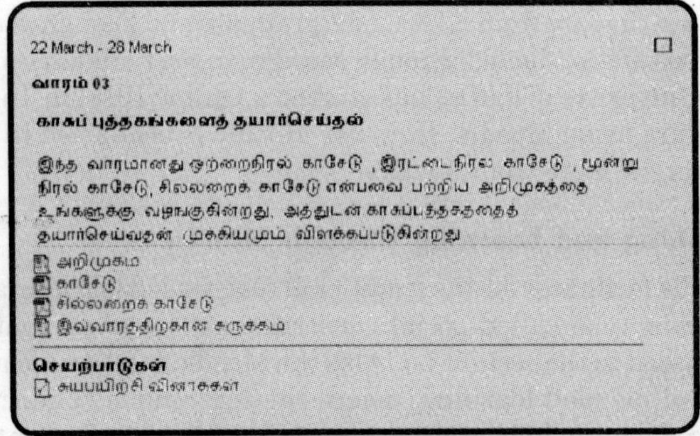

Fig. 11.1 : Resources view in Moddle.

Likewise in social constructivist learning point of view also these resources can be used to share knowledge of learners and help constructing knowledge.

Activities

In addition to the resources, activities are another main part of Moodle. Assignments, Wiki, Choices, Forum, Lessons, Quizzes and Surveys are some of the activities that are used in Moodle. In teacher led learning these activities are used to assess learners.

On the other hand these activities are used as a medium to construct knowledge in social constructivist learning. The learners can collaboratively participate in Forums, Wiki, Blogs etc. and share their experiences and knowledge with peers to construct knowledge. The facilitators can monitor activities and administrate activities.

Other Collaborative Features

Moodle has chat and email to interact among peers and teachers. In addition to that anyone can maintain a blog and update their profiles so that they can get to know each other. Also there is a calendar to manage the events and in which we can keep global events and personal events.

Reporting and Monitoring

Moodle has very rich monitoring mechanism through which every single action of users can be monitored. We can track from which IP the user is logged in and what are the pages viewed and what are the actions performed during the visit. In addition that Moodle shows the recent events when a users log in and that help one to check what has happened recently.

Administration and Security

User administration, Course administration and System administration can be easily done in Moodle. Under user administration we can create and administrate users as well as we can control the enrollments. Since Moodle is a web based system the security considerations have been taken well. A usage policy, user privileges customization, automatic backups, secure logins etc. can be managed and maintained.

Methodology

As Moodle is a Learning Management System, users can only interact with courses. Therefore before start any lessons, a course need to be created.

Next the teachers who are responsible for the course should be assigned. Teachers have over all control of the courses and they can perform all the actions as they like. In terms of e-Learning they are called as facilitators, not teachers. The actual responsibility of the facilitator is to make the course and facilitates learners so that the learners can easily interact with each other and construct knowledge. After that the relevant learners should be assigned to the course. Users even can be further grouped inside a course so that they can be managed easily.

Next create relevant activities so that learners can interact with each other and share knowledge. The activities should be created so that when learners can follow them and the intended learning objectives and knowledge can be achieved. In addition to that the facilitators should monitor and check whether information overloading and unnecessary knowledge sharing are happening.

Recent Developments

Virtual worlds may useful in future to conduct and practical oriented courses via online. Soodle [7] is an effort to have the Moodle installed in Virtual worlds and connect it with real world Moodle instants. Nowadays people have started buy lands in virtual worlds and many vendors have even started their online stalls in virtual worlds. Moodle also has stepped in to that and many researches going in these directions.

Further many the activities, like role play, are still not possible in Moodle. The next major release of Moodle is Moodle 2.0 and it has many improvements including more support for collaboration, security, web services, repository managements etc.

Conclusion

Moodle is a good tool for collaborative learning. The young Tamil generation is more interested in social networking and virtual collaborations. Therefore the collaborative learning which is facilitated by Moodle Learning Management System may help them to learn Tamil language efficiently and effectively.

REFERENCES

1. http://en.wikipedia.org/wiki/Pedagogy, Accessed on 20100420.
2. Brooks, J. and Brooks, M. (1993). *In Search of Understanding: The Case for Constructivist Classrooms*, ASCD.
3. http://docs.moodle.org/en/Philosophy, Accessed on 20100320.
4. http://en.wikipedia.org/wiki/Elearning, Accessed on 20100420.
5. http://uoj.nodes.lk, Accessed on 20100520.
6. http://demo.moodle.net/course/view.php?id=615, Accessed on 20100520.
7. http://www.sloodle.org/moodle/, Accessed on 20100520.

12

Morphological Generator for Tamil

A New Data Driven Approach

— *Rekha R.U.*
— *Anand kumar M.*
— *Dhanalakshmi V. Soman*
— *Rajendran S.*

ABSTRACT

Tamil is morphologically rich language. Being agglutinative language most of the categories expressed are suffixes. Tamil is a post positional inflectional language it has more suffixes compared with English. The Morphological Generator takes lemma and a morpho-lexical description as input and gives a wordform as output. It is a reverse process of Morphological Analyzer. Morphological generator system implemented here is a new data driven approach which is simple, efficient and does not require any rules and morpheme dictionary. We have developed an individual system to handle nouns and verbs. Any automated machine translation system requires morphological analyzer of source language and morphological generator of the target language. Using this morphological generator we also developed a verb conjugations and noun declension. Here Tamil verbs are classified into 32 paradigms [1] and 1500 word forms are handled. Like verbs nouns are classified into 25 paradigms and 325 word forms are handled. An inflection table is arranged in Two Dimensional format where row corresponds to the morpho-lexical form and column corresponds to the paradigm number. The noun inflection table contains 325 rows (word forms) and 25 columns (paradigms) similarly verb inflection table contains 1500 rows (word forms) and 25 columns (paradigms).

Introduction

Natural Language Processing (NLP) has been developed in 1960. The aim of NLP is studying the problems in the automatic generation and understanding of natural languages. The primary goal is to build computational models of natural language for its various analysis and generation. Tamil verbs are inflected into several grammatical features. In Tamil language the verb specifies almost everything like gender, number, and person markings and also with auxiliaries it represents mood and aspect. These are the morphological information of the root words. This makes a challenging work in Tamil. In general in Indian language there are many inflections compared to other languages. Morphological generator generates a word form from a lemma, word class, and the type of morpholexical inflection required. In Tamil language some time the root word undergoes morphological change when it attaches to the inflection. Morphological generator can be an individual module or integrated with several NLP applications like machine translation, Automatic sentence generation. In this paper we describe a fast and simple morphological generator for Tamil. This novel approach can be applied to any morphologically rich languages.

Morphological Generator for Tamil

Generally, morphological generator tool is developed using

rule based approach. Where the rule based approach requires a set of morphosyntactic rules, spelling rules and morpheme dictionary. In this novel approach rules and dictionaries are not required it only requires the inflection table and paradigm classifier programme. Here, the morphological generator receives an input in the form of lemma+word_class+ morpho-lexical Information, where lemma specifies the lemma of the word form to be generated, word_class specifies the grammatical category (noun/verb) and morpho-lexical Information specifies the type of inflection.

In this section we describe the files used in the data creation and the algorithm for the implementation of this system. A Perl programme is written for finding the paradigm and index number it makes this system simple and efficient. The algorithm of this method is described in the below sections.

Creation of Inflection Table

Number of paradigms for each word class (noun/verb) is defined. In Tamil; there are 32 paradigms for verb and 25 for noun. For every paradigm a word is selected this is termed as head word. For this head word all word form is created, in Tamil there are more than thousand word forms are possible for a head word. Here we have selected 1500 most frequently used word forms for verb including auxiliary& clitics and for noun it is 325 including postpositions. This verb/noun word form creation uses an order which is followed for all the paradigms. A morpholexical Information list is also created for the above word forms.

Using all the word forms a table is created each column of the table corresponds to its paradigm. For each column remove the stem. This table is converted into a tabular CSV format and represented as an inflection table. Table 12.1 represents the sample data for Tamil verbs. In this table row indicates the Morpholexical inflection and column indicates paradigm number.

Table 12.1 : Inflection table for Tamil Verbs

		Paradigm number						
		1	2	3	4	5	....	32
Morpholexical Inflection	1	ththAn	inAN	NdAn	ddAn	RAn		
	2	ththAL	inAL	NdAL	ddAL	RAL		
	3	ththAR	inAR	NdAR	ddAR	RAR		
	4	ththOm	inOm	NdOm	ddOm	ROm		
	:							
	:							
	1660							

Input Format: Lemma + word class – morpholexical Information

Example: padi + V + PAST_3SM = padithththAn.

maram + N + ACC_Marker = maraththai.

Algorithm Developed for Morphological Generator

Input Format: Lemma + word class + morpho-lexical Information

Out format: Word = MORPGEN (Input)

```
MORPGEN (Input)
l, w, m = SPLIT (Input)
rl = ROMAN (I)
parnum = PARNUM (rise)
colindex = parium
rowindex = INDEX (in.to)
inflection = INFTABLE [rowindex] (colinex]
stem = STEM (l, iv, pariun)
words = JOIN (stem inflection)
end
```

where,

l is the lemma

w is the world class

m is the morpho-lexical information

rl is the romanized lemma

SPLIT: This function split the users input into as lemma, word class and morpho-lexical information.

ROMAN: It romanizes the lemma part.

PARNUM: This function identifies the paradigm number using romanized lemma and word class

INDEX: This retrieves the index of morpho-lexical inflection from the morpho-lexical inflection file

INFTABLE: Using the row and column index the inflection part is retrieved from the inflection table.

STEM: Taking romanized lemma and paradigm number as input it gives the stem.

JOIN: It concatenates the stem and inflection part.

Methodology

The whole system is divided into two modules. Module-I handles the lemma/root part and Module-II handles the morpho-lexical information. In Module-I the lemma/root word in Unicode format is romanized and the paradigm number is identified by end characters. A simple PERL programme is written for finding the paradigm umber. The identified paradigm number is referred as *Column Index* and stemming is also performed using this paradigm number. In Module-II the Morpho-lexicon information is given as an input. A complete set of Morpho-lexicon information are stored in a file with index numbers.

The index number of the corresponding input is identified. This refers the *Row Index*. A verb and noun inflection tables are used in this system. In this Two-Dimensional inflection table rows are Morpholexical information index and columns are paradigm numbers. For each paradigm we have created a complete set of morphological inflections corresponding to the morpholexical information. Finally using the column index and row index morphological inflection is retrieved from the inflection table. This inflected form is affixed with the stem. In this work a morphological generator is designed for each of the syntactic categories and then combined to morphologically generate a complete sentence.

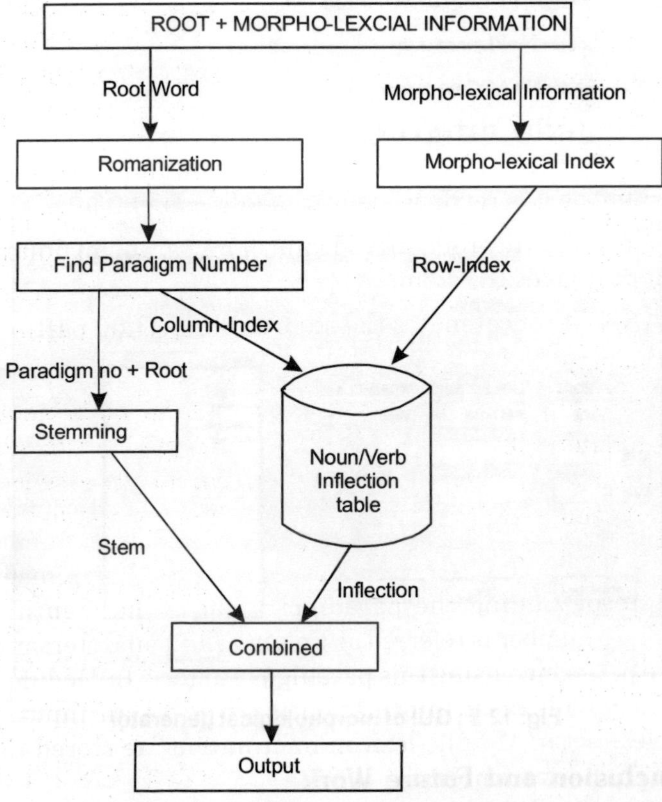

Fig. 12.1 : Morpholigical Generator System

In this system we also handled some difficult tasks. First one is where a lemma has more than one possible surface word form given a particular morpho-lexical inflection type and word class. Second is where a surface word has more than one possible morpho-lexical inflection type. The gui snapshot for the morphological generator is shown in figure 12.2.

Examples:

படி + V + PAST_3SH = படித்தார்/படிந்தார்

ஓடு+ V + PAST_3SF = ஓடினாள்

சா(கு)+V+ PAST_3SM =செத்தான்

மரம்+N+PL=மரங்கள்

முள்+N+ACC=முள்ளை

பூ+N+PL_DAT=பூக்களிற்கு

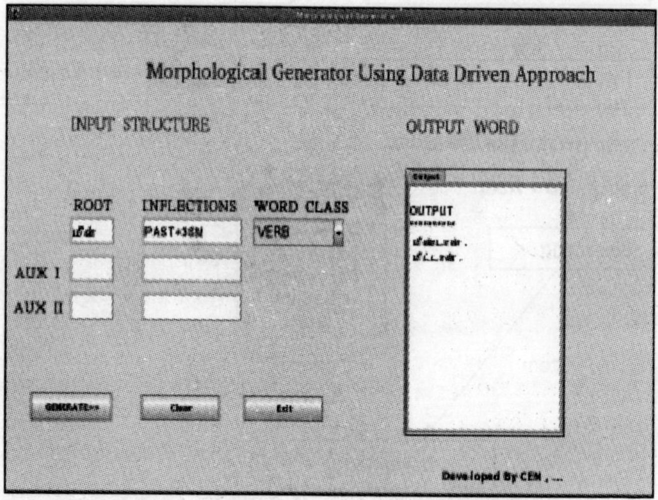

Fig. 12.2 : GUI of morphological generator

Conclusion and Future Work

Morphological generator which is explained here is a novel approch. It is developed using a very simple and efficient method. This is not a language specific method so this can be applicable for all the morphologically rich languages. Using this approach currently we are developing morphological generator for Malayalam and Telugu. This system provides a vast application it's used in noun declension, verb conjugation, automatic sentence generator and also in featured this system is unique handles auxiliaries and clitics, it does not require any spelling rules and this methodology can be implemented for any language. This work can be further used for implementing morphology based translation system between any language to Tamil.

REFERENCES

1. Rajendran, S., Arulmozi, S., Ramesh Kumar, Viswanathan, S. 2001. *Computational Morphology of Verbal Complex*, Languageirundia Volume 3 : 4 April 2003.
2. Guido Minnen, John Carroll, and Darren Pearce, 2000. *Robust Applied Morphological Generation.* In Proceedings of the First International Natural Language Generation Conference, pages 201-208, 12-16 June.
3. Ganapathiraju, Madhavi and Lori Levin: TelMore: *Morphological Generators for Telugu Nouns and Verbs.* In the Proceedings of Second International Conference on Universal Digital Library Alexandria, Egypt November 17-19, 2006.
4. Anadnan, P, Rajani Parthasarathy, Geetha, T.V. 2001. *Morphological Generator for Tamil* in Tamil Internet 2001 Conference Proceedings, Malaysia.

13

FaceWaves
A Tamil Text to Video Framework

— *Madhan Karky*
— *T. V. Geetha*
— *Ravi Varman*

ABSTRACT

This paper presents FaceWaves, a framework for interactive information interchange for Tamil Internet and mobile users. A text-to-video subsystem for generating faces and animating them purely based on textual descriptions is proposed. Using textual descriptions to create a face by describing the visual features of a person and animating their face to speak out given information, can provide an efficient means of storing/transferring an animated video. The Text-to video subsystem comprises of a morphological analyser, ontology of facial features and expressions, Tamil text to speech, lip synchroniser, and emotion handler. To best of our knowledge, this is the first framework proposed for interactive information interchange with sophisticated language technology tools such as text to speech, text to video and voice to text. This framework facilitates storing and transferring video files over a network as plain text and converting the text to a video with a lightweight local client. This paper describes various components of the framework and shows the results from text-to-face generation module. The paper concludes discussing the results, opening a new area for the Tamil computing research community.

Introduction

Increasing number of Internet users, exponentially growing content and limited available bandwidth [1] has always been a problem to the Internet community. The number of information sources in Tamil and the number of Tamil users who contribute and consume is increasing every hour with the advent of blogs, microblogs and social networks. Almost every Tamil newspapers around the world now have their own portals feeding news and articles in Tamil every hour. We see bots collecting news from multiple sources and summarising the news. Auto-Journalists are already collecting sports scores from a website and generating a full fledged human like report about the match discussing performance of players purely based on numbers. Tamil is very soon going to adapt to these new growing technologies.

We foresee the need for human like auto-reporters who can read out a given news article, or can summarize any information source. We foresee the need for virtual faces that can listen to user queries and respond with answers. We foresee a system that can create a set of characters, backdrops and animate them from plain Tamil textual descriptions. In this paper we propose FaceWaves, a framework that enables creating such videos that can be transferred over any network as plain text and converted to video using a lightweight local client. This framework provides an ideal platform for transferring videos across world wide web and also in mobile networks.

This paper is organised into five sections. The second section discusses the background and motivation of this paper with related literature. The FaceWaves framework and components are given in section three. Section four provieds the results from our face generator module of the FaceWaves framework in detail with snapshots from our GUI. The fifth section concludes the paper with our work in progress and future research in this domain.

Background

Tat Seng et al., proposed a animation sequencing method from text which tries to build 3D animations from a manual [2]. The proposed system tries to capture the concepts from the manual and extracts the features to provide the user with the option of choosing between textual or graphical modes. Narichika et al., in 2009 proposes a similar system that generates a movie from a script to a TV like programme [3]. In this work the authors describe a framework that creates agents and a prototype that demonstrates controlling the generated agents. We find this work closely related to our proposed FaceWaves framework with respect to creating agents from text. A few Tamil Text-to-speech systems exist [2,6,7] and FaceWaves uses an improved variation of a text to speech system presented in [2]. Tamil speech to text has various proposals such as [3] and a fully working system yet to be demonstrated. Detecting emotions from a given text has been carried out in different languages [9-11] and the FaceWaves framework proposes an emotion identifier and applying emotions on a computer-generated face.

FaceWaves Framework

Face Waves architecture comprises of three main components. Information System, Wave Processor and Language Tools. An Interface Manager will be developed as a web tool, integrating all services to be accessible by clients. The components of the system are described briefly in the following sections.

(a) Information System

Information System is responsible for crawling textual information on various topics over a structured information architecture such as Wikipedia (Tamil). The crawled information is processed and conceptually indexed using CoRe, a concept and relation based indexing system for large text collections.

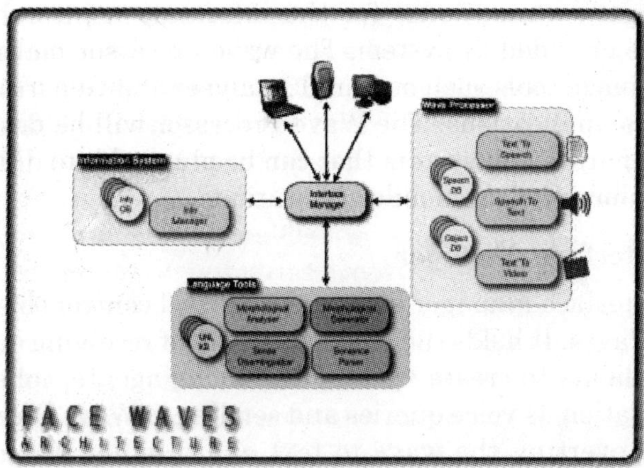

Fig. 13.1 : FaceWaves Framework.

One key advantage of such an method would be to have a language independent indexing. The Information Manager will be responsible for crawling, processing, enconverting Tamil text to Universal Networking Language graphs, indexing the concept graphs, ranking documents based on concepts, retrieving and formatting results as requested by the Interface Manager.

(b) Language Tools

Language Tools subsystem offers Tamil language dependent services such as morphological analysis, generation, named entity recognition, word sense disambiguation and sentence parser. These tools will be integrated into a system as a service for Wave Processor and Information System.

(c) Wave Processor

Wave processor comprises three major units. Text to Speech, Speech to Text and Text to Video. These units work independent of each other and output of one unit can be piped as input to the other. The key responsibility of this system is to provide interaction elements (speech, agents, and agent animations) for the information interchange service provided by system. The wave processor makes use of language tools such as Tamil Analyser and Generator for various applications. The Wave Processor will be designed as a separate sub-system that can be plugged into different standalone, web or mobile applications.

(d) Interface Manager

The interface manager acts as the central control object for FaceWaves. It holds the responsibilities of receiving queries from clients to create agents, displaying agents, collecting information as voice queries and sending to Wave Processor and converting the wave to text and sending the text to Information system to retrieve information and resend the information to Wave Processor to convert them to speech and agent animation and finally to play the animation video on the client's interface.

Text to Video Subsystem

The Text to Video subsystem of FaceWaves framework, as depicted in figure 13.2, comprises of a Document Processor, Face Generator, Backdrop Selector, Emotion Processor and a Movie Manager.

A plain text, semi-structured script file comprising of character descriptions, scene descriptions and dialogues is processed by Document processor to extract the corresponding sections and formats them structurally and routes the corresponding formatted information to Face generator, Backdrop selector and Emotion Processor. The face generator uses a face description ontology to describe dimensions of different parts of the human face for the given description. Backdrop selector uses a background library and analyses the scene description to rank and choose appropriate background for the given scene.

Emotion Processor analyses the text and tags the dialogues with appropriate emotions using an Emotion ontology. The Face description, selected backdrop and annotated dialogues are then sent to the Movie manager which produces a plain text movie description file which can be sent back to the client. A lightweight movie player in the client on receiving the Movie Description, processes the description and uses a Tamil Text to Speech module and synchronises the lip movements with the generated speech and face with appropriate emotion with the selected backdrop. The Movie Player generates a full length running animation movie with synchronised subtitles.

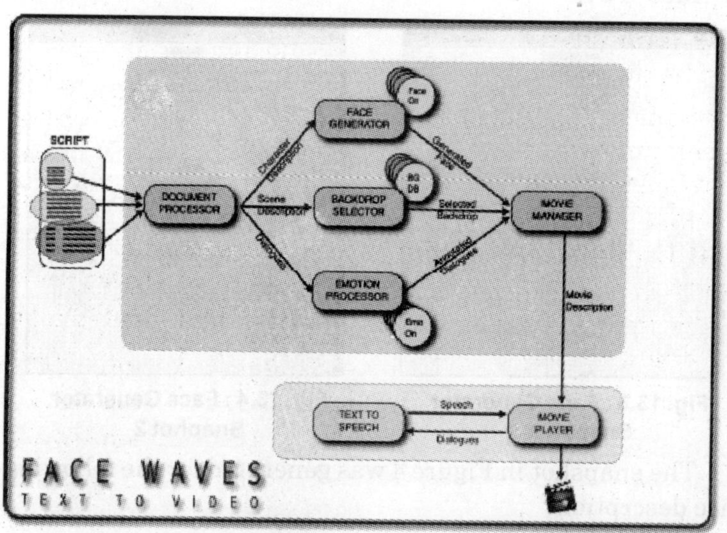

Fig. 13.2 : Texts to Video Subsystem

Results : Face Generator

This section discusses the Face Generator module and how plain text Tamil descriptions are converted to a human face. The Face Generator module as explained in the previous section uses a face description ontology along with a Morphological Generator.

A sample face description can be in a free flowing form such as

> ஆதி அடர்த்தியான புருவங்களும் நீளமான மூக்கும் அகண்ட கண்களும் சிறிய உதடுகளும் கொண்டிருந்தான்
>
> aadhi adarthiyaana puruvangaLum neeLamaana mookkum aka.Nda kankaLum stRiya uthadugaLum koNdirunthaan
>
> Aadhi has thick eyebrows, long nose, big wide eyes and small lips

The image generated for the face description provided above is provided in figure 13.3 as a snapshot from our text-to-video GUI.

Fig. 13.3 : Face Generator Snapshot 1

Fig. 13.4 : Face Generator Snaphot 2

The snapshot in Figure 4 was generated for the following face descrption.

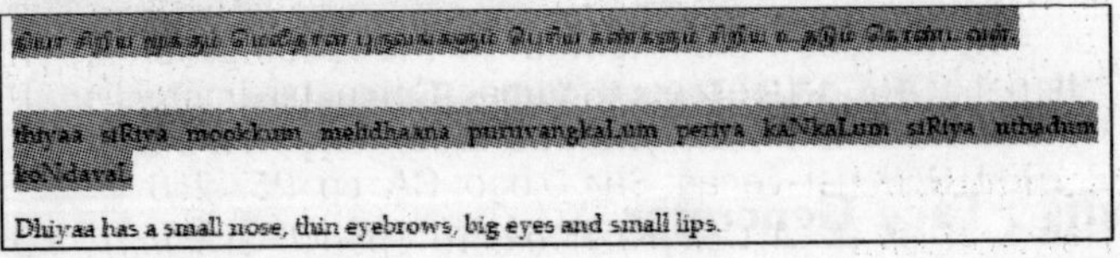

தியா சிறிய மூக்கும் மெலிதான புருவங்களும் பெரிய கண்களும் சிறிய உதடும் கொண்டவள்.

thiyaa siRiya mookkum melidhaana puruvangkaLum periya kaNkaLum siRiya uthadum koNdavaL

Dhiyaa has a small nose, thin eyebrows, big eyes and small lips.

The face generator module was developed in Java. The generator gets the face description text as input and uses a morphological analyser, sentence parser and face description ontology to retrieve the facial features from the given descriptions. A neutral face is initially described as a collection of objects one for each part of the face. The member variables of each object, which define the dimension of the corresponding part of face, are modified based on the adjectives describing each part in the face description.

Conclusion and Future Work

The current face generator module does not take into account the descriptions for hair, skin colour and texture, moustache, special marks or any three dimensional descriptions. Including these features in the face generation module will be our future work along with integrating the face generation module with adding expressions to the face based on the emotion identified from the dialogue. This paper provides the overall FaceWaves framework and describes one particular subsystem, Tamil text-to-video, and one key module of the subsystem, Face Generator. We believe that this paper will open numerous research problems for the Tamil computing community.

REFERENCES

1. Anandan, R. Parthasarathi, and Geetha, *Morphological Analyser for Tamil*. ICON 2002, 2002.
2. Karky, M., *et al. Tamil Voice Engine*. in INFITT. 2001, Malaysia.
3. Lakshmi and H. Murthy. A Syllable based continuous speech recognizer for Tamil. in *ICSLP*. 2006. Pittsburgh: Interspeech.
4. Marketing, M., World Internet Statistics, http://www.internetworld stats.com/stats.htm. 2009.
5. Narichika, H., *et al.*, User-Definable Rule Description Framework for Autonomous Actor Agents, in Proceedings of the 13th International Conference on Human-Computer Interaction. Part III: Ubiquitous and Intelligent Interaction %@ 978-3-642-02579-2. 2009, Springer-Verlag: San Diego, CA. pp. 257-266.
6. Rama, J., *et al., A Complete Text To Speech System in Tamil*. IEEE, 2002.
7. Rao, N., *et al.* Text-to-speech synthesis using Syllable-like Units in National Conference on Communications, 2005. Kharagpur, India.
8. Tat-Seng, C. and L. Thiam-Beng, From Text Description to Animation Sequences, in Proceedings of the Computer Animation %@ 0-8186-7588-8. 1996, *IEEE Computer Society*. p. 175.

Context Based Information Search for Thirukural

— *N. Ilakiyaselvan*

ABSTRACT

Thirukural is a discourse on the art of living, a set of healthy principles of guidance for the variety of segments of the civilization for a pleasant-sounding combined living. Each episodes and couplet (kurals) in Thirukural are related to the real time world. In the Tamil language "Thiru" means "holy" or "sacred," and "Kural" means anything that is brief or short. This paper focuses on context based searching for Thirukural and describes the techniques of Natural Language Processing (NLP) which is to design and build software that will analyze and apply in both understanding and generating natural languages that humans use naturally. A fundamental phenomenon of natural language is the variability of semantic expression. The system should understand the short story of some sentences like paragraph and result kurals with given relative meaning. Based on the given context, it retrieves the information of couplets (kurals) with the ranking priority. The system identifies the relative terms and using the term frequency calculates the weightage for each terms.

Keywords: *Thirukural, Natural Language Processing, Couplets, Semantic expression, Term frequency.*

Introduction

In this information search is based on the Natural Language Processing. NLP is a field of computer science and linguistic concerned with the interactions between computers and human natural languages. Two fields of NLP are: Natural language generation, system converts information from computer database into readable language and Natural language understanding, system converts human language into computers known format. The system participating in this competition must do something more than the system from other NLP competitions: to prove capabilities of understanding how language works. Same meaning can be expressed by, or inferred from different texts mapping between language expressions and meanings. Humans use different expressions to convey the same meaning. Therefore, numerous NLP applications, such as, Question Answering, Information Extraction. Summarization require computational models of language that recognize the semantic approach. Trying to capture the major semantic inferences needed to understand equivalent semantic expressions. There are several levels of the meaning of the texts, ranging from shallow level to deep one. But, it is still difficult to make a consensus on how to describe the deep meaning. In Question and Answering, an indexing is considered as the predictive annotation.

Text Meaning : Representation forms the Tamil dictionary which contains extended relative meanings. Information Retrieval must be started when the queries enters for searching couplets.

Literature Survey

In Natural Language Processing, denotes as "Understanding" language means, among other things, knowing what concepts a word or phrase stands for and knowing how to link those concepts together in a meaningful way [6]. Basically Communication between Human and the system starts from Question and answering [3] and the main goal of QA is, whenever the user types a question, system must produces the correct answer. The Challenge is to analyze the questions, gathers information and presents the answer.

Question and answering is also related to text summarization technology [4], it contains short questions and answers. Sometimes there will be no answer for questions or multiple answers for questions, which have no answer object in documents to a given question or there are many answer objects. When a new question comes up, the system compares it with all the questions in the library and finds the most detailed standard question to match it. Then the corresponding answer is returned to the user [2].

While in Information Retrieval, An efficient indexing mechanism is normally used to quickly retrieve the information. And [7] Question Answering and information Retrieval are the two candidates of Natural Language Processing. An Indexing is used for searching, or finding the respective information. And the meaning represents the TMR language [1], which is the knowledge representation system for representing text meaning. An Onomasticon, or lexicon is nothing but the collection of proper names and terms; a dictionary.

Thirukural plays an important role of our human life[8] and the Greatness of Thirukural is a precious gem among the classics, unique in the deliverance of code of conduct to the mankind to follow for all time to come. This poem consisting of 133 sections of 10 couplets each which was predictable as a masterpiece of ancient literature in Tamil in its own times, has stood the test of history and is established by posterity as a decisive work which has predisposed the thoughts of man throughout the centuries. It is not only of great artistic and stylistic literary value, but also a direct to the art of living with pieces of precious wisdom.

How the Search Engine Works

The context based Information search can be obtained by identifying the relativity among terms and derive a context from the terms. The term ranking can be calculated using Term frequency in the given sentence or paragraph of words.

Users query could be answered in semantic approach and get the couplets in ranking order. The above architecture diagram clearly explains the flow of the paper. The system gets the input text as sentences like paragragh for searching information. The given sentence or paragraph is tokenized and each token is passed to Tamil language analyzer. The analyzer identifies the part of the syntax such as noun, verb, adjective, pronoun, adverb and so on that the token belongs to.

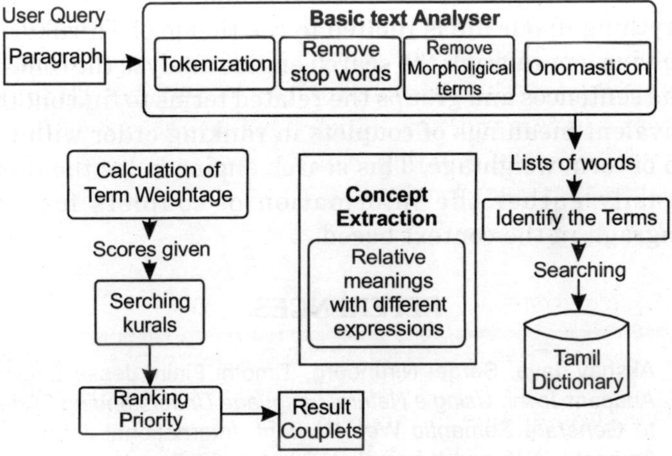

Fig. 14.1 : Overall Architecture

The analyzer removes the common Tamil morphological. The system uses the noun, verb, adjective and adverbs to find the relation among the terms. The relativity among the terms can be derived using a Tamil dictionary. The term weightage is calculated for each relative term using the term weightage formula. The context is extracted from the relative terms and finally searches the couplets in a Thirukural database.

Term Weightage Formula

By using Term Weightage Formula, calculates the weightage of the words which could be in any form as related meaning, different expression and comparative meaning. In a paragragh some of the sentences have same meaning but in different expressions by using term weightage formula, a well formed questions term having the weightage.

Conclusion

Thirukural is a treatise par excellence on the art of living and the real greatness of Thirukural is its survival, even after the onslaughts of many heterogenous creeds. Each and everything in our life is related to the theme of Thirukural. By giving a paragragh the search engine analyse the context of the sentences and groups the related terms to find out the equivalent meanings of couplets in ranking order with the help of term weightage. This search engine helps the users to easily gather the information of couplets for any paragragh in the context based.

REFERENCES

1. Akshay Java, Sergei Nirunburg, Timothi Finin, Jesse English, Anupam Joshi, *Using a Natural Language Understanding System to Generate Semantic Web Content*, International Journal on Semantic Web and Information System, 2007.
2. Fuji Ren and Tianjiao Gu, *Question Matching based on Fuzzy Set*, Faculty of Engg., The University of Tokushima, IEEE International conference, 2008.
3. Jamie Callan, *Human Language Technologies, Open Domain Question Answering*, Carnegie Mellon University, 2004.
4. Jun'ichi FUKUMOTO, Tsuneaki KATO, *An Overview of Question and Answering Challenge (QAC)*, Ritsumeikan University IEEE, 2002.

5. Mitsuru Ishizuka, *A Common Concept Description of Natural Language Texts as the Foundation of Semantic Computing on the Web*. The University of Tokyo.
6. Natural Language Processing, "http://research.microsoft.com/en-us/groups/nlp".
7. Thorsten Brants, *Natural Language Processing in Information Retrieval*, 2003.
8. "Tamil Virtual University" enable Tamil Education Easily and Effectively.
9. " http://www.tamilvu.org".

Computational Approaches for Learning Inflections in Tamil

— K. Rajan
— V. Ramalingam
— M. Ganesan

ABSTRACT

This paper proposes machine learning techniques for the study of inflections in Tamil. In recent years there has been growing interest in using machine learning techniques for natural language processing tasks. Recent computational research on natural languge corpora has revealed that simple machine learning mechanisms could make an important contribution to certain aspects of language acquisition.

There are regularities that can be captured mechanically, by exploiting distributional patterns found in the language data. Very large corpora will yield to mathematical model of language systems. The Artificial neural network (ANN) is used to learn the regularities of Tamil morphology. In this paper, the methods of feature extraction and feature representation for Tamil verb morphology are discussed. The ANN network with three layers is trained with the features extracted from different verb conjugations generated by the morphological generator. More than 7800 word forms are used for training and testing this model. The network produces the grammatical values as output for the morphemes present in the given word. This model does not require morphological rules. The output is comparable with the results of rule based morphological analyser. The performance of this model on different verb types is presented.

Keywords: *Machine learning, Tamil morphology, ANN Language Model.*

Introduction

In recent years there has been growing interest in using machine learning techniques for natural language processing tasks. In this paper, the artificial neural network is trained to learn the relationship between the morphemes and their categories from the training set of inflected Tamil verb forms. Morphemes are portions of a word that recur in other words with the same meaning. They are minimal, that they cannot be broken into pieces. The grammatical value of the whole word is related to the component morphemes of the word. In highly-inflecting and compounding languages the number of possible word forms is very high. This poses special challenges to Natural Language Processing systems dealing with these languages.

The morphological tagging is an important problem in the area of computational linguistics, as it underlies other crucial tasks such as syntactic parsing and machine translation. Artificial neural network is a promising approach to this kind of problem, for which the exact algorithmic solution is unknown or not efficient enough. In this paper we present the results obtained by the application of neural network model trained with back propagation algorithm for Tamil morphology. Knowledge discovery in text is a non-trivial process of identifying valid, novel, potentially useful, and understandable patterns in unstructured text data. Learning algorithms are an integral part of knowledge discovery. Learning techniques may be supervised or unsupervised. Supervised learning techniques enjoy a better success rate as defined in terms of usefulness of discovered knowledge (Maciej Majewski, 2008). Machine learning is the capacity of a computer to learn from experience (*i.e.*, data) and to extract knowledge from examples. A successful learner should be able to make general conclusions about the data it is trained on. This allows it to act appropriately in new situations.

Related Works

The supervised learning of morphological rules is based on the annotated data as the alignment of orthographic words with their morpheme representations. In order to apply supervised learning methods, the data should further be extended with information about inflectional classes and features (part-of-speech tags), thus making the output of the training mechanism compatible with the input for morphological analysers.

There is unsupervised learning of morphological rules. The advantage of unsupervised morphological learning is that it requires only the set of orthographic words (completely "raw data") without any stem/affix lists or grammatical annotation. However, most of the unsupervised methods put restrictions on the number of morphemes per word, on rule complexity etc. The goal of these methods is merely splitting a word into stem and suffix without the capability of assigning any grammatical information. A number of unsupervised learning techniques have been applied: genetic algorithms (Kazakov, 1997), a minimal description length approach based on spelling of words and the set of suffixes that appear with each stem (Goldsmith, 2001), and the quasi-roots algorithm (Sheremetyeva and Nirenburg, 1999).

Many researchers have been working on similar morphological learning systems for Indian languages. One of the earlier rule based morphological analyser was developed for Tamil at CIIL (Ganesan M, 1994), S.R. Kolhe and B.V. Pawar have investigated the inductive inference of grammar of subset of Marathi, Pradipta Ranjan Ray presented a computational model for Bengali Morphological analysis using Finite State methods. A generic architecture for morphological generators of agglutinative languages has been proposed (Uma Maheshwar Rao. G., 2006), in which corpus is used to extract fully inflected word forms. Stochastic taggers like HMM will not give a high accuracy for Tamil because the language is inflectionally rich and is relatively free-word order (Arulmozhi *et.al* 2006). In their paper, they have discussed the algorithm for developing a rule based tagger for Tamil. No work has been reported on machine learning techniques using Artificial neural network for morphology of Indian languages. ANN is applied for text reasoning (Maciej Majewski *et.al*, 2008), Natural language processing tasks (Joao Luis Garcia Rosa, 2002),(J.L Elman, 1990), (Ahmed, 2002), (Rajan K *et.al,* 2002), (Quing Ma, 2003) and categorization of Tamil Documents (Rajan K. *et. al*, 2009).

Tamil Morphology

The Tamil morphology is characterised as agglutinative or concatenative. That is, morphs are agglutinated or concatenated in a sequence after a stem. Concatenative morphology in Tamil involves always suffixation (Thomas Lehman, 1993). This is represented as Stem + (affix) where the superscript n means one or more occurrences of a suffix. Morphs are concatenated as suffixes at the right of a word stem, to produce inflected or derived forms of words. In Tamil, there is another morphological process which is reduplication. All lexical or root morphemes are grouped into four major types. They are verbal, nominal, adjectival and adverbial roots. All other types of words can be identified as an inflected or uninflected form of these stems. Nouns can be inflected for the case and number. An inflected noun form may be the realisation of three morphemes, as given in the following representation.

Noun stem + [Plural suffix] + [Oblique] + [Case suffix]

Verbs can be inflected for tense, person, number, gender and others.

Verb stem + [Tense Marker] +[Verbal Participle Suffix] + [Auxiliary verb] +[Tense Marker]+[Person, Number, Gender].

Post positions and adjectives cannot be inflected. The derivation occurs only in nouns. When morphemes or words combine, certain morphophonemic changes occur. Nouns can be inflected for the case and number. Inflected verbs in Tamil are finite or non-finite. Finite verbs mark both tense and subject-verb agreement, non-finite verbs do not. Finite verbs occur only in restricted contexts in the structure of a sentence; they typically mark the end of a sentence.

The lexical knowledge is characterised with respect to verbs. All the grammatical information that is, about tense, number, gender, etc is carried by the verbs in a sentence. These are the reasons why the study of verbs has acquired immense importance in Linguistics. Modern Tamil has three tenses. Each tense morpheme is realised by a number of tense suffixes or allomorphs. Tense suffixes are listed in Table 15.1.

Table 15.1 : Tamil tense markers

Tense	Suffixes
Present	kiR, kkiR, kinR, kkinR
Past	t,tt,ndt,in,inR
Future	p,v,pp

The sccond inflectional suffix after the stem is a PNG marker. The Table 15.2 shows the person, number and gender suffixes.

Table 15.2 : Tamil PNG markers

op	Number	Gender	Suffix	
First	Singular		Een	
	Plural		Oom	
Second	Singular		Aay	
	Plural		Iirkal	
Third	Singular	Masculine	aan	Aar
		Feminine	aaL	
		Neuter	Atu	
	Plural	Masculine/ Feminine	aarkaL	
		Neuter	Ana	

Tamil distinguishes between 4 types of non-finite verb forms. The non-finite verb forms, except the infinitive have both positive and negative forms. Only the adjectival participle distinguishes tense. All other non-finite verbs are tense less. Each of the non-finite verb forms is marked with a non-finite verb suffix, which is added to the verb stem, or to the tense suffix. The infinitive is formed by the affixation of infinitive suffix to the verb stem. The conditional verb form occurs both in a positive and negative forms.

Table 15.3 : Non-Finite verb sufixes

Non-Finite	Suffixes	
Infinitive	~a	
Adj Participle	t,tt,ndt,in,inR kiR, kkiR, um	~a
Verbal Participle	t,tt,ndt,in	~u ~t
Conditional	~aal,~aaviTTaal	

This is formed by adding the phoneme cluster of the past tense allomorph to the verb stem and then affixing the conditional suffix (-aal/-aaviTTal). Adjectival participle is formed by adding past or present tense allomorphs to the verb stem and the adjectival suffix (-a).

The suffix ~um morph realised the future tense morpheme and the adjectival morpheme. It is an instance of homophony of morphs in Tamil.

Neural Network

Artificial neural networks are computational models based on biological neural networks. They can be used to model complex relationship between inputs and outputs or to find pattern in data. Neural network based approaches learn the associations of word-to-tag mappings, from a training data set and also generalise to unseen examples. Neural networks have self learning capability, are fault tolerant and noise immune.

In this paper, a three layer feed forward neural network with hyperbolic tangent (tanh) function is used in hidden layers followed by a linear output layer. The neural network is trained using backpropagation algorithm. A momentum term is used to achieve a faster global convergence. A bias value is used to enable each neuron to fire hundred per cent.

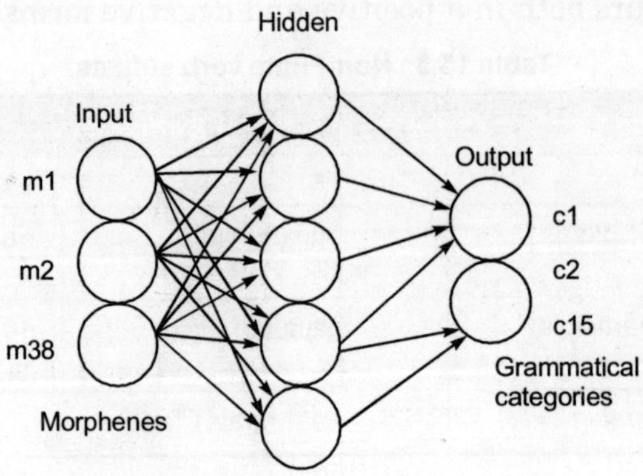

Fig. 15.1 : Architecture of ANN model

The input layer is used to represent the 38 morpheme features of the input word. The output layer represents the grammatical values of the cluster of morpheme features. The structure of the ANN model is **38 L – 30 N – 15 L**, representing the number of neurons/units in the input layer, hidden layer and the output layer respectively. The letters L and N denote linear and non-linear activation functions. In this study, the network is trained with a learning rate of 0.01 and 2000 epochs.

Feature Extraction

The input and output vectors are prepared from the word-forms generated from 208 Tamil verb stems using the morphological generator. The verbs are inflected for tense, person, number and gender. They are also inflected for non-finite forms. During the process of generating the various conjugations, their corresponding grammatical categories are also collected as output. The stems are combined with different morphemes of various categories by the generator. The morpheme table has 38 features. The categories are marked for 15 grammatical values according to the morpheme components added with the stem. This method has been utilised because, the corpus may not have all the combinations. Totally 7800 different word forms have been generated and stored in the form of input and output vectors. Among the 7800 samples, 5000 samples are randomly selected for training. The network is tested by using the remaining list of 2800 samples.

The binary representation of input and output vectors are created for all word-forms by scanning through all morphemes. The morphemes are listed in the descending order of their length. If a particular morpheme is found within the word-form, it is represented by 1 in the input vector and also the corresponding category value is set to 1 for the output vector. During testing phase, only the input vectors are created from the given word-form. The feature vector for the word is given by equation 1.

w = { m1,m2,m3,...,mn} ——————_ 1

The word w is a sequence of n morphemes

Where mi = 1 if i th morpheme is present in the word w., otherwise 0.

The input feature extraction from word forms during the test phase is same as the one followed during the training.

Results and Discussions

The proposed model of supervised learning for Tamil morphology shows the ability of neural networks to learn the morpheme to category association.

Table 15.4 : Performance of the ANN Model

Number of test Samples	Numbers correctly recognized	Precision
Total 2800	2694	96.21%
Finite Verbs 1900	1863	98.13%
Non-Finite Verbs 900	829	92.11%

The system produces correct categories for the morpheme sequences of all the inflected forms of finite verbs that are not part of the training set. The non-finite forms shows lower recognition rate because of the shorter morphemes than for the finite verb forms. The Table 15.4 shows the performance of the model on these two verb types.

Conclusion

The proposed neural network model is a powerful supervised machine learning system that can be applied effectively for any inflectional morphological language. This approach is cost effective, because it does not require any explicit grammar rules. The experimental result shows its promising performance for morphologically rich languages like Tamil. This work can be extended to cover other grammatical categories of Tamil, by changing the input and output vectors of the neural network.

REFERENCES

1. Ahmed, S. Bapi Raju, P.V.S. Chandrasekhar, M. Krishna Prasad, 2002. *Application of Multilayer Perceptron Network for Tagging Parts-of-Speech*. Proceedings of the Language Engineering Conference (LEC'02), IEEE Computer Society: 57-63.
2. Arulmozhi P, Sobha L and Kumara Shanmugam B. 2004. *Parts of Speech Tagger for Tamil: Symposium on Indian Morphology. Phonology & Language Engineering*, March 19-21. IIT Kharagpur. 55-57.
3. Elman J.L., 1990, Finding Structure in Time.. *Cognitive Science* 14 : 179-211.
4. Ganesan.M. 1994. *A Scheme for Grammatical Tagging of Corpora in Indian Languages*. B.B. Rajaprohit (Ed.), CIIL.
5. John A. Goldsmith, 2001. *Unsupervised Learning of the Morphology of a Natural Language*. Computational Linguistics, 27(2):153{198.)
6. Kazakov, D., 2000. *Achievements and Prospects of Learning Word Morphology with Inductive Logic Programming*. In Cussens & Dzeroski (Ed.), Learning Language in Logic. : 89-109.
7. Rumelhart D.E , J. L. McLelland, 1986. *On Learning Past Tenses of English verbs*. In D. E.Rumelhart and J. L McLelland, Editors, Parallel Distributed Processing, Volume 2, pages 216-271. MIT Press, Cambridge, MA.
8. Rajan.K, Ramalingam.V, Ganesan M 2002a. *Corpus Analysis and Tagging: Symposium on Translation Support System*. IIT, Kanpur.
9. Rajan.K, Ramalingam.V, Ganesan M 2002b, *Applications of Neural Network for Tamil Studies : Proceedings of the International Conference on Tamil Computing*. Chennai, India: Univerity of Madras.
10. Thomas Lehman. *A grammar of Modern Tamil*, 1993. Pondicherry Institute of Linguistics and Culture.

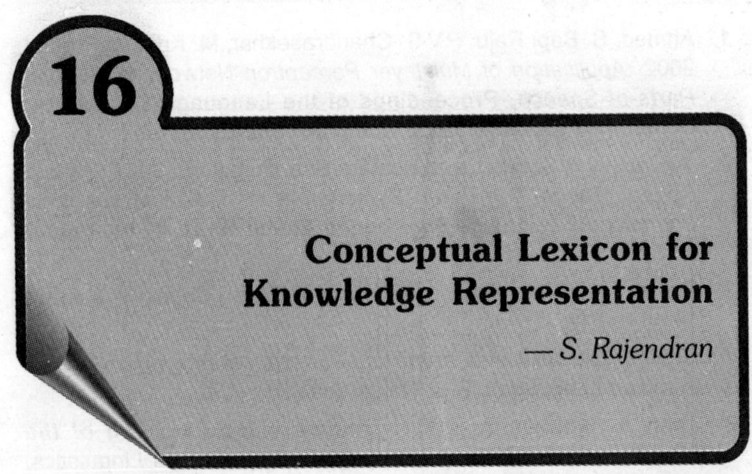

16

Conceptual Lexicon for Knowledge Representation

— S. Rajendran

Introduction

Conceptual graphs emphasize semantics. The earliest forms, called existential graphs, were invented by the philosopher Chrales Sander Peirce (1897) as a graphical notation for symbolic logic. Lucien Teniere (1959) used similar graphs for his dependency grammar. The earliest form implemented on a computer was the correlational nets by Silvio Cecato (1961), who used them as intermediate language for machine translation. There are philosophical and psychological evidence that conceptual graphs are mental representation unbounded by knowledge of a particular language.

The proposed conceptual lexicon has concepts as its entries which are independent of a specific language and the meanings of concepts are given in terms of conceptual graphs from which the surface representation of lexical items belonging to a particular language can be derived. The proposed lexicon can be manipulated to generate a text in the form of a target language. The theory propounded by Sowa (1984) has been exploited to suit our purpose. At the same time the four levels of representations proposed for the a generative lexicon (Pustejovsky, 1995) and the semantic representation in WordNet (Pike Vassion, 2000) are also kept in mind while writing the meaning of a lexical item by means of conceptual graph.

Why Conceptual Lexicon

Dictionary definitions are mostly inadequate representations of words or concepts. A real definition will become encyclopedic. Let us take the concepts "horse" and "book". "Horse" may require at least the following representation:

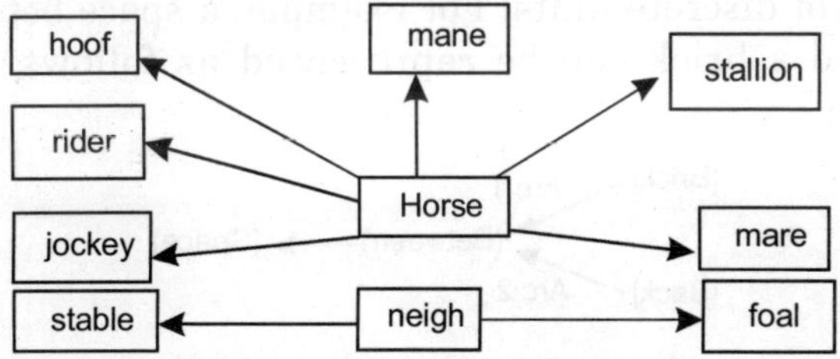

Similarly "book" requires the following represenation:

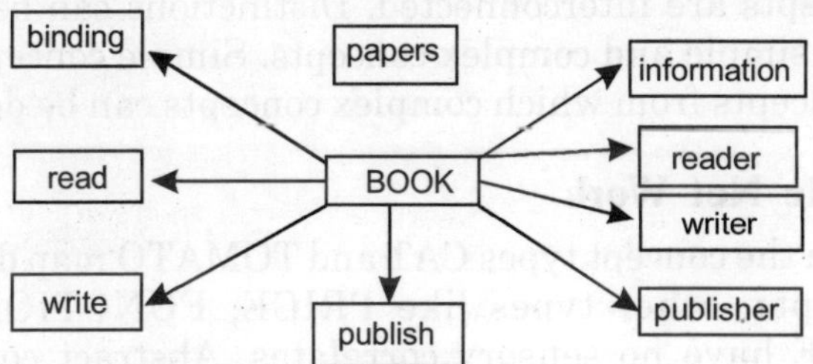

For a universal representation of concepts across languages conceptual graphs may be used.

Conceptual Graphs

Conceptual graphs from a knowledge representation language based on linguistics, psychology and philosophy

(Sowa, 1984: 69). Concepts are language independent ones derived form percepts. A conceptual graph is a finite, connected, bipartite graph. The two kinds of nodes of the bipartite graph are concepts and conceptual relations. Every conceptual relation has one or more arcs, each of which must be linked to some concept. If a relation has n arcs, it is said to be n-adic, and its arcs are labelled 1, 2,...n. The term monadic is synonymous with 1-adic, dyadic with 2-adic and triadic with 3-adic. A single concept by itself may form a conceptual graph, but every arc of every conceptual relation must be linked to some concept. Concepts are discrete units. Combinations of concepts are not diffuse mixtures, but ordered structures. Only discrete relations are recorded in concepts. Continuous forms must be approximated by patterns of discrete units. For example, a space between a brick and a brick can be represented as follows (Sowa, 1984:72):

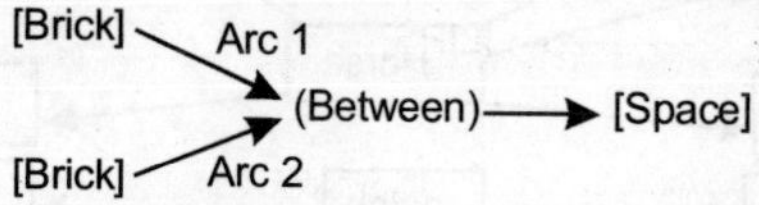

In the graphs, concept nodes represent entities, attributes, states, and events, and relation nodes show how the concepts are interconnected. Distinctions can be made between simple and complex concepts. Simple concepts are basic concepts from which complex concepts can be derived.

Semantic Net Work

Although the concept types CAT and TOMATO map directly to percepts, other types like PRICE, FUNCTION and JUSTICE have no sensory correlates. Abstract concepts acquire their meanings not through direct associations with percepts, but through a vast net works of relationship that ultimately links them to concrete concepts. A conceptual graph has no meaning in isolation. For example, the description of the concept, MAN is represented as follows:

[MAN] □(ISA) □[HUMAN BEING] □(ISA) □[ANIMAL]

Abstraction and Definition

Definition can specify a type in two different ways: by stating necessary and sufficient conditions for the type, or by giving a few examples and saying that everything similar to these belongs to the type. The first method derives from Aristotle's method of definition by genus and differentiae. And the second method is closer to Wittgenstein (1953). AI systems have supported both methods. Conceptual graphs support type definitions by genus and differentiae as well as schemata and prototypes. Type definition for KISS (Sowa, 1984:106)

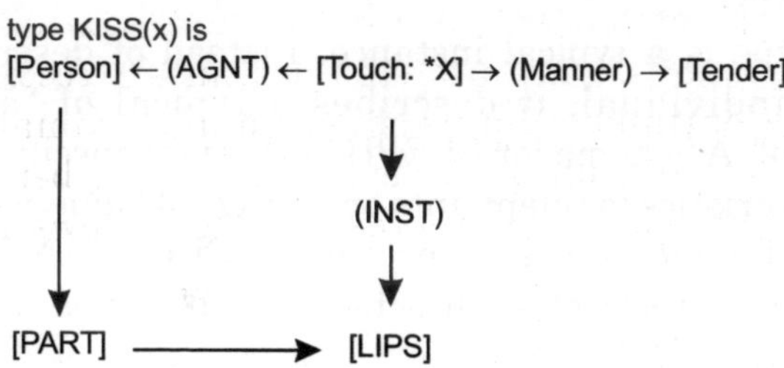

Schemata

The basic structure for representing background knowledge for human-like inference is called the schemata. It is a pattern derived form past experience that is used for interpreting, planning, and imagining other experiences. Schemata incorporate domain-specific knowledge about the typical constellations of entities, attributes and events in the real world. Schemata are similar in structure to type definition. Yet concept type may have at most one definition, but arbitrarily many schemata. Type definitions present the narrow notion of a concept, and schemata present the broad notion. Type definitions are obligatory conditions that state only the essential properties, but schemata are optional defaults that state the commonly associated accidental properties.

Schemata show the typical ways in which a concept may be used, but they do not describe a typical instance of a concept.

Schema for BUS (x) is (Sowa, 1983: 129)

```
[BUS] ← (INST) ← [TAVEL] → (RATE) → [SPEED:< 60 kmsph]
  ↑     ↘
(OBJ)     (CON)
  ↑           ↘
[DRIVE]          [PASSENGER: (*)]
  ↓                    ↓
[AGNT]               (QTY)
  ↓                    ↓
[DRIVER]           [NUMBER = 50]
```

Prototype

A prototype is a typical instance. Instead of describing a specific individual, it describes a typical of "average individual". A Schema for ELEPHANT might specify a range of characteristics for elephants or a range of behaviours and habitats for elephants. A prototype ELEPHANT would combine and restrict such schema to describe a typical elephant.

Proto type for ELEPHANT (x) is (Sowa 1984: 136):

```
[ELEPHANT: *X]—
        (CHAC]  →  [HEIGHT: @ 3.3 M]
        (CHAC]  →  [WEIGHT: @ 5400 KG]
        (COLR)  →  [DARK-GREY]
        (PART)  →  [NOSE]–
                   (ATTR) → [PREHENSILE]
                   (IDNT) → [TRUNK]
        (PART)  →  [EAR] (*)]–
                   (QTY) → [NUMBER: 2]
                   (ATTR) → [FLOPPY]
        (PART)  →  [TUSK: (*)] –
                   (QTY) → [NUMBER: 2]
                   (MATR) → [IVORY]
        (PART)  →  [LEG: (*)]
                   (QTY) → [NUMBER: 4]
        (STAT)  →  [LIVE]–
                   (LOC) → [CONTINENT: (Africa/Asia)]
                   (DUR) → [TIME: @ 50 YEARS]
```

Conceptual Representation

Some of the conceptual relations listed in Sowa (1984) are adopted to suit our purpose.

- accompaniment. (ACCM) links [ENTITY:*x] to [ENTITY:*y] where *y is accompanying *x.
- agent. [AGNT] links [ACT] to [ANIMATE], where ANIMATE concept represents the actor of the action.
- attribute. (ATTR) links [ENTITY:*x] to [ENTITY:*y] where *x has an attribute *y.
- cause. (CASE) links [STATE:*x] to [STATE:*y] where *x has a cause *y.
- characteristic. (CHRC) links [ENTITY:*x] to [ENTITY]
- destination. (DEST) links [ACT] to [ENTITY] towards which the action is directed.
- experience (EXPR) links [STATE] to [ANIMATE], who is experiencing that state.
- instrument. (INST) links [ENITY] to [ACT] in which the entity is causally involved.

The following relations are also taken in to account to define a concept using some other concept.

Hypemymy-Hyponymy		Animal → Mammal
Hyponymy-Hypemymy		COW → MAMMAL
Holonymy-Meronymy	Wholes to parts	TABLE → LEG
	Groups to members	DEPARTMENT → PROFESSOR
Meronymy-Holonymy	Parts to wholes	WHEEL → CART
Troponymy	From events to their subtypes	WALK → LIMP
Entailment	From events to the events they entail	SNORE → SLEEP

Pustejovsky (2001:56) characterize a generative lexicon as a computational system involving at least the following levels of representation:

1. ARGUMENT STRUCTURE: Specification of number and type of logical arguments
2. EVENT STRUCTURE: Definition of the event type of an expression and its subeventual structure
3. QUALIA STRUCTURE: A structural differentiation of the predicative force for a lexical item
4. LEXICAL INHERITANCE STRUCTURE: Identification of how a lexical structure is related to other structures in this type of lattice Pustejovsky (2001:56) assumes that word meaning is structured on the basis of four generative factors, or qualia roles, that capture how humans understand objects and relations in the world and provide the minimal explanation for the linguistic behaviour of lexical items.

CONSTITUTIVE: the relation between an object and its constituent parts

FORMAL: the basic category that distinguishes the object within a larger domain

TELIC: the object's purpose and function

AGENTIVE: factors involved in the object's origin or "coming into being."

The qualia structure is the core of the generative properties of the lexicon, because it provides a general strategy for creating increasingly specific concepts with conjunctive properties. A simple schematic description of a lexical item, □, using this representation is shown below:

The lexical structure for book as an object can then be represented as follows:

A
ARGSTR = ARGI = x
...

CONST = what x is made of
QUALIA = FORMAL = what x is
TELIC = function of x
AGENTIVE = how x come into being

The lexical structure for book as an object can then be represented as follows:

book
ARGI = y information
ARGSTR = ARG2 = xphys_obj
information.phy_obj
FORM = holds (x, y)
QUALIA = TELIC = read (e, w, x, y)
AGENT = write (e, v, x, y)

The ideas propounded by Pustejovsky will also be taken into consideration while defining a concept.

The following is the sample of the conceptual lexicon. Each item is a concept and the concepts will be mapped against the lexical items of a language.

[CAT] → [ISA] → [ANIMAL]
[PENCIL] → (ISA) → [INSTRUMENT)
↓
(FUNCT)
↓
[WRITING]

The verbs are provided with argument structures. A frame of arguments will be given with their necessary relations. The verbal concept ACT represented in the following fashion.

[ACT] (ISA) → [EVENT)
(AGENT) → [ANIMATE ENTITY]
[ARRIVE) (ISA) → [EVENT)-
(AGENT) → [MOBILE-ENTITY]
(GOAL) → [LOCATION]

Lexical and Conceptual Structures

Each natural language has a well-organized lexical and syntactic system. Each domain of knowledge has a well-organized conceptual system. Complexities arise because each language tends to use and reuse the same words and lexical patterns in many different conceptual domains. The lexical structures are

- Relatively domain independent,
- Dependent on syntax and word forms,
- Highly language dependent.

And the conceptual structures are

- Highly domain dependent,
- Independent of syntax and word forms,
- Language independent, but possibly culture dependent.

When there are cross-linguistic similarities in lexical patterns, they usually result from underlying conceptual similarities. English verb give, for example, takes a subject, object, and indirect object. Other languages may have different cases marked by different prepositions, postpositions, inflections, and word order; but the verb that mean roughly the same as give also have three participants – a giver, a thing given, and a recipient. In all languages, the three participants in the conceptual pattern lead to three arguments in the lexical patterns.

The distinction between lexical structures and conceptual structures addresses the following things:

- Lexical structures are oriented towards language. The representation developed here is strongly influenced by linguistic theories of syntax and thematic roles.
- Conceptual structures are designed for representing knowledge about the world. They may grow too large to be expressed in a single sentence, and they may contain concepts types that cannot be expressed by a single word.

- Since they can be represented by similar structures, the same operations can be used on them. Furthermore, lexical structures can be converted to deeper conceptual structures by a step-by-step process, not by a translation between radically different forms.
- Finally, common structures facilitate language learning and conceptual creativity. In learning, a child generalizes conceptual structures learned form experience to form the initial lexical structures needed for language. Metaphor and conceptual refinement create new conceptual structures by adapting old lexical structures to novel situations.

Conclusion

The distinction between lexical structures and conceptual structures provides a principled basis for partitioning knowledge into the lexicon and the more detailed knowledge about the world. Conceptual graphs provide formalism for representing both kinds of structures with a level of precision that allows deeper and more systematic analysis of the relationship between them. As a result, they can help to replace vague discussion with a precise methodology that has a greater chance of being computerized.

Finally the direct mapping between conceptual graph and natural language can simplify the task of knowledge acquisition: a knowledge base of conceptual graphs could be generated directly form natural language inputs. After being primed with a dictionary of lexical knowledge, the system could build up its own encyclopaedia of world with the aid of a tutor communicating in English, not a knowledge engineer coding in a specialized notation.

REFERENCES

1. Bouillon, P and Busa, F. 2001, *Qualia and the Structuring of Verb Meaning*. In: P. Bouillon and F. Busa (eds.). The Language of Word Meaning. Cambridge: Cambridge University Press, 149-167.

2. ———2001. *Type Construction and the Logic of Concepts*. In: P. Boulillon and F. Busa (eds). Language of Word Meaning. Cambridge: Cambridge University Press, 91-123.
3. Busa, F & Calzolari, N and Lenci, A. 2001. *Generative Lexicon and the SIMPLE Model: Developing Semantic Resources for NLP*. In: P. Boulillon and F. Busa (eds). Language of Word Meaning. Cambridge: Cambridge University Press, 333-349.
4. Cruse, D.A. 1986. *Lexical Semantics*. New York: Cambridge University Press.
5. Grimshaw, J. 1990. *Argument Structure*. Cambridge: MIT Press.
6. Foddor, J.A. and Lepore, E. 2001. " *The Emptiness of the Lexicon: Critical Reflections on J. Pustejovky's* "The Generative Lexicon." In: P. Boulillon and F. Busa (eds). Language of Word Meaning. Cambridge: Cambridge University Press, 28-49.
7. McGilvary, J. 2001. *Chomsky on the Creative Aspect of Language Use and Its Implications for Lexical Semantic Studies*. In: P. Boulillon and F. Busa (eds). Language of Word Meaning. Cambridge: Cambridge University Press, 5-27.
8. Pustejovksy, J. 1994. "*A Richer Characterization of Dictionary Entries: The Role of Knowledge Representation*." In B.T.S. Atkins, and A. Zampolli (eds.). Computational Approach to Lexicon. Oxford: Oxford University Press.
9. ———1995a. "*Linguistic Constraint on Type Coercion*." P. Saint-Dizoer and E. Viegas (eds.). Computational Lexical Semantics. Cambridge: Cambridge University Press.
10. ———1995b. The Generative Lexicon. Cambridge, Massachusetts: The MIT Press.
11. ———2001. "*Generativity and Explanation in Semantics*: A Reply to Fodor and Lepore." In Language of Word Meaning. Cambridge: Cambridge University Press, 51-74.
12. Peirce, C.S. 1960. *Collected papers of Charles Sandrers*. Peirce. Arthur W. Burks(ed.) 8 vols., Cambridge: Harward University Press.
13. Pustejovky, J. and Boguraev, B. 1993. "*Lexical Knowledge Representation and Natural Language Processing.*" In: F. Pereira and B. Grosz (eds.), Natural Language Processing. Cambridge, Mass.: MIT Press.
14. Rajendran, S. 1978. *Syntax and Semantics of Tamil Verbs* (manuscript). Ph.D. Thesis. Poona: University of Poona.

15. ———1983. *Semantics of Tamil Vocabulary*. (Report of the UGC sponsored Postdoctoral Work in manuscript). Poona: Deccan College Post Graduate and Research Institute.
16. ——— 2002. "*Preliminaries to the Preparation of a Word Net for Tamil.*" Language in India 2:1, www.langugeinindia.com
17. ——— 2003. "*Creating Generative Lexicon from Dictionaries: Tamil Experience.*" In: Recent Advances in Natural Language Processing: Proceedings of the ICON 2003. Myore: CIIL, 83-91.
18. ———2004. *Priorities in the Pursuit of Preparing a Generative Lexicon for Tamil.* Paper read in ICOIL held in CASL, Annamalai University.
19. Rajendran, S., Arulmozi S., Kumara Shanmugam, B., Baskaran, S. and Thiyagarajan, S. 2002. "*Tamil WordNet.*" In Proceedings of the First International Global WordNet Conference. Mysore: CIIL, 271- 274.
20. Ruimy, N. Gola, E. and Monachini, M. 2001. *Lexicography Informs Lexical Semantics: The SIMPLE Experience*. In P. Boulillon and F. Busa, (eds). Language of Word Meaning. Cambridge: Cambridge University Press.
21. Saint-Dizoer, P and Viegas, E. (eds.) 1995. *Computational Lexical Semantics*. Cambridge: Cambridge University Press.
22. Somers, H.L. 1987. *Valency and Case in Computational Linguistics*. Edinburgh: Edinburgh University Press.
23. Sowa, J.F. 1984. *Conceptual Structures: Information Processing in Mind and Machine*. Reading: Addison-Wesley Publishing Company.
24. ——— 1988. "*Using a Lexlcon of Canonical Graphs in a Semantic Interpreter.*" In M. Evens (ed.) Relational Models of the Lexicon. New York: Cambridge University Press, pp 73-97.
25. —— 1993. "*Lexical Structure and Conceptual Structures.*" In: Semantics and the Lexicon.
26. Dordrecht: Kluwer Academic Publishers.
27. Sowa, J.F. and Eileen, C.W. 1986. "*Implementing a Semantic Interpreter for Conceptual Graphs.*" IBM Research and Development 30 (1), 57-69.

Noun Phrase Chunker using Finite State Automata for an Agglutinative Language

— Vijay Sundar Ram R.
— Sobha Lalitha Devi

ABSTRACT

This paper presents a system for noun phrase chunking for Tamil, an agglutinative language. The partial chunking of the text is done by a rule-based approach where the rules are embedded in a finite state automaton (FSA), which recognizes the chunks at a high accuracy rate and speed. The chunking of text being the pre-processing task needs to be of good performance. The evaluation of the system shows a recall of 93.7% and precision of 94.9%.

Introduction

We present a system for noun phrase chunking for an agglutinative language, Tamil. The noun phrase considered here has a head noun preceded by determiner, quantifier, classifier and adjective in sequence. Here the determiner, quantifier, classifier, and adjective are optional. The recursive noun phrase occurs when possessive case marker occurs. Often the noun phrase has the information about the happening. The event executor and event receiver of the event are usually noun phrases around the verb. The proper chunking of noun phrase helps in improving the efficiency of the information extraction, machine translation and in information retrieval system by improving the terms in the term vs document matrix.

The system is built using rule based approach, where the rules are embedded in a finite state automaton (FSA), as the structures are recognized with high degree of accuracy. Several methods have come up for this task. Church's stochastic noun phrase tagging was one of the early attempts, where the corpus frequencies were used to determine the noun phrase boundaries (Church, 1988). Abney did partial parsing using finite state cascades, where the finite state cascade has sequence of levels. Phrase at one level is built on the phrase at the previous level without any recursion (Abney, 1996). Ramshaw and Marcus used Eric Brill's transformation based learning for recognizing the noun chunks and other text chunking (Ramshaw, 1995). Dimitrios Kokkinakis and Sofie Johansson Kokkinakis did a cascaded Finite-State Parser for Syntactic Analysis of Swedish (Dimitrios, 1999). Chunk tagger using markov model technique for recognizing the internal structures and syntactic category of simple as well as complex structures was done by Wojciech (Wojciech 1998). Noun phrase chunking for German using probabilistic context-free parser for learning and tagging the most probable chunk sequence is done by Helmut (Helmut, 2000). The rest of the paper is organised as follows. The section 2 starts with briefing about the agglutinative language with samples of noun phases. In section 3 techniques of finite state automata (FSA), different preprocessing works and the implementation of the Tamil NP chunker are explained. The evaluation and the discussions on result in section 4 and finally the paper ends with conclusion.

Description about the Language

The system is developed for an agglutinative language such as Tamil, Telugu, Malayalam, etc. Here the language under consideration is Tamil. Tamil belongs to the South Dravidian family of languages. It is a verb final language and allows scrambling. It has post positions, the genitive precedes the head noun in the genitive phrase and the complementizer follows the embedded clause. Adjective, participial adjectives and free relatives precede the head noun. It is a nominative-accusative language like the other Dravidian languages. The subject of a Tamil sentence is mostly nominative, although there are constructions with certain verbs that require dative subjects. Tamil has png agreement.

Noun Phrases in Tamil

Tamil is a relatively free word order language, but when it comes to noun phrases and clausal constructions it behave as a fixed word order language. As in other languages, Tamil also has optional and obligatory parts in the noun phrase. Head noun is obligatory and all other constituents that precede the head noun are optional. In this section we discuss in detail about different noun phrases in Tamil. Consider the following:

1. periya viitu
   big+ADJ house+N+NOM
   (Big House)
2. oru azhakiya viitukku
   one +Q beautiful+ADJ house+N+DAT
   (For a beautiful house)
3. inta koyil
   this+DET temple+N+NOM
   (This temple)

In examples 1, 2 and 3 the structure of the noun phrase has a head noun, which may or may not be preceded by optional categories like determiner, quantifier, classifier, and adjective. This is the general structure of noun phrase. This structure is represented by the following Rule.

Rule a:

NP=>[Determiner][Quantifier][classifier] [Adjective] {N}

4. avanutaiya bramaandamaana araiyin vizakukal His+PN+POS grand+ADJ

room+N+POS lamp+N+PL

(His grand room's lamp)

Example 4 has a possessive noun. If the head noun has a possessive case marker and followed by a noun phrase, both the noun phrases are chunked into one noun phrase. This may go recursively. This is shown in Rule b.

Rule b:

possessive NP => [Determiner][Quantifier][classifier] [Adjective] {N+possessive case}

NP=> (possessiveNP)* Rule a

The rule a and b are combined into a single rule

Rule 1:

NP=> [possessive NP] +Rule a

5. ivviitu

this+DET house+N+NOM

(This house)

Here compounding of the determiner and the noun forms single word. The tags of this word also obey the previous rule but the tags are in the same word. This type is handled separately to accept the tags within the word.

6. powuc ceyalaalar
(Secretary)

In example 6, here the two nouns, which are suppose to be a single noun is written separately and connected by a sandhi. This is handled by the rule given below:

Rule 2:

NP=> {N+sandhi} {head N}

7. therku maaligai

south+N+NOM palace+N+NOM

(Southern palace)

Example 7 has two nominative nouns, where the first denotes the direction. These two nouns go together to form a noun phrase. The eight directions north, south, east, west, northeastern, northwestern, south-eastern and south-western are considered. This is handled by the following rule

Rule 3:

NP => {direction denoting NP} {NP}

8. kadal niir

sea+N+NOM water+N+NOM

(Seawater)

When two nominative nouns are adjacent to each other the two nominative nouns can be chunked into noun phrase.

NP => {N+NOM} {N+NOM}

Tamil NP Chunker

The noun phrase chunking is done by building finite state automata using the linguistic rules. By traversing the text through the FSA, the chunking of the text is done.

Finite State Automata A finite state automaton is an abstract device used for recognizing simple syntactic structures or patterns in text strings. An automaton is normally depicted by a directed graph in a so-called state diagram. An FSA as a string-processing device accepts text strings as input and decides if the structure is correct, that is, it either accepts or rejects the string. From a mathematical point of view, it may therefore be regarded as a function, mapping a set of strings to the set {ACCEPT, REJECT}. Based on the transitions given by the FSA, they are classified as Non-Deterministic Finite State Automata (NFA) and Deterministic Finite State Automata (DFA).

The deterministic FSA is found to be unsuitable for parsing of the sentence. Since the grammar of the languages are context free and non-deterministic in nature. But for partial chunking such as noun phrase chunking the structure of the phrase are highly fixed. So usage of deterministic FSA helps in high degree of accurate chunking.

The Deterministic Finite-State Automaton (DFA) which is a special case of NFA has the following requirements:

1. There are no transitions involving e.
2. No state has two outgoing transitions based on the same symbol

The Deterministic FSA used in this task is shown in Figure 17.1.

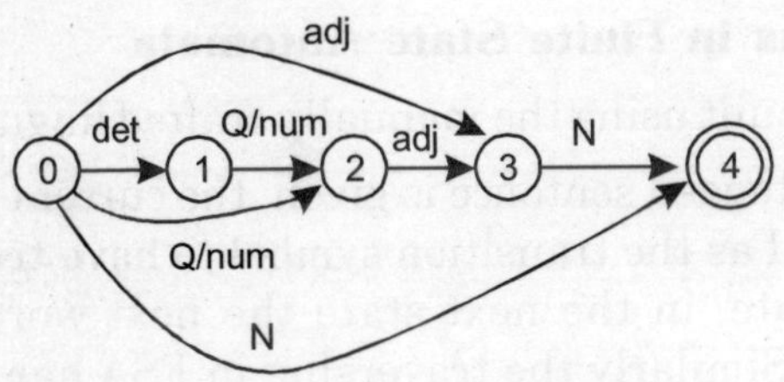

Fig. 17.1 : Deterministic FSA

In the present work the FSA is used in the form of a state table. The morphological tags of the words are the transition symbols.

Architecture of the System

The architecture of the system is shown in Figure 17.2.

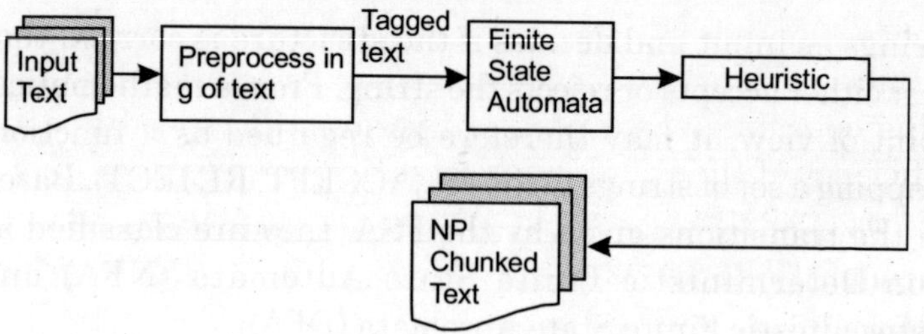

Fig. 17.2 : Architecture

The Preprocessing Works

The input text to be chunked is initially fed to the morphological analyser (Viswanathan 2003), which gives multiple outputs for each word. The morphologically tagged output is sent to a hybrid approach based Part of Speech (POS) tagger (Arulmozhi 2006), where the ambiguities in the output of the morphological analyser are corrected using the POS tags.

On giving the preprocessed text, which is now a tagged text, state transition takes place in FSA based on the tags as the symbol to trigger the transition. The chunking of the phrase completely depends on the morphological tags.

The Process in Finite State Automata

The FSA is built using the manually crafted linguistic rules.

When a tagged sentence is given, the current word's tag is considered as the transition symbol to have transition to the next state, in the next state the next word's tags is considered. Similarly the traversing in FSA happens till it reaches the end state. If it successfully reaches the end state this part of the text is chunked as noun phrase.

The nouns with all the case markers have the same noun phrase structure except the nouns with possessive case marker. So the nouns with all case markers except the possessive case marker are treated similarly. So the case marking tags in the nouns except the possessive case are not considered. This suppression of the sub-tags reduces the number of transition from 400 to 40 in the determinized FSA. This optimizes the FSA and improves the speed and the efficiency of the chunking process.

The noun phrase chunked text obtained after traversing through the FSA, is again processed using the heuristic rules.

Results and Discussion

The system is evaluated with the data taken from the CIIL corpus (Central Institute of Indian languages corpus). The numbers of sentences under consideration are 500, which contains 2180 noun phrases. The Input Text Preprocessin g of Text Finite State Automata Heuristic NP Chunked Text Tagged text number of noun phrases recognized correctly by the system is 2043, which is at a precision of 94.9% and the recall of 93.7%. The results are tabulated as follows.

Table 17.1 : Performance of the Chunker

Sl.No.	Number of Sentences	Number of NPs present	Number of chunked	Number of NPs correctly chunked	Recall %	Precession %
1.	300	2180	2153	2043	93.7	94.9

The capitalization of the first letter gives an easy identification of proper nouns in English language. This is not there in Indian languages, which makes the task of recognizing the noun phrase complex. The challenging task is chunking the noun phrase formed by two nouns such as "kadal niir"(sea water), which should be recognized as one chunk. We cannot go blindly by chunking two nominative nouns into a chunk because doing that will make error in the following case.

raman	palam	saappittaan
raman+N+NOM	fruit+N+NOM	eat+V+PST

(raman ate fruit)

Here if we apply the rule that two adjacent nominative nouns will form a chunk, then the two nouns 'raman' and 'palam' will form as one chunk, "raman palam". But this is an incorrect chunk since they are two different noun phrases where 'raman' is the subject and 'palam' is the object of the sentence. The accusative marker, the marker of direct object, in 'palam' is dropped which is a common phenomenon in Tamil. We are trying to over come this by subcategorizing the verb to identify the subject and object of the verb. These types of correction have to be done after the chunking is over.

Conclusion

The paper presents a noun phrase chunking for an agglutinative language, Tamil. In developing the system we are using finite state automata technique, where the rules are embedded in it. The system performs with 94.9% precession and 93.7% recall. The system takes 2.5 sec to chunk 1000 sentences. In future, we will be handling the noun phrases with multiple nouns.

REFERENCES

1. Steven Abney (1996). *Partial Parsing via Finite-State Cascades.* In Proceedings of the ESSLLI '96 Robust Parsing Workshop
2. Arulmozhi Palanisamy and Sobha Lalitha Devi. 2006. *HMM based POS Tagger for a Relatively Free Word Order Language*, Journal of Research on Computing Science, Mexico. 18: 37-48.
3. Dimitrios Kokkinakis and Sofie Johansson Kokkinakis 1999. In Proceedings of EACL'99, Bergen.
4. Kenneth W. Church, 1988. *A Stochastic Parts Programme and Noun Phrase Parser for Unrestricted Text.* In Proceedings of the Second Conference on Applied Natural Language Processing.
5. L. Ramshaw and M. Marcus, 1995. *Text Chunking using Transformation-Based Learning.* In Proceedings of the Third Workshop on Very Large Corpora.

6. Helmut Schmid and Sabine Schulte im Walde 2000. *Robust German Noun Chunking With a Probabilistic Context-Free Grammar*. In Proceedings of COLING 2000, Saarbrucken.

7. Wojciech Skut, Thorsten Brants (1998), *Chunk Tagger Statistical Recognition of Noun Phrases*. In the Proceedings of ESSLLI-1998 Workshop on Automated Acquisition of Syntax and Parsing. Saarbruucken, Germany.

8. Viswanathan, S Ramesh Kumar, B Kumara Shanmugam, S Arulmozi 2003, *A Tamil Morphological Analyser*, International Conference on Natural Language Processing, Central Institute of Indian Languages, Mysore.

9. Dr. Steve Sugden http://www.it.bond.edu.au/inft150/033/lectures/ch10.pdf

18

Animated Sangathamizh Poems
E-Learning

— Arul Natarajan

Introduction

This paper on Animated Sangathamizh poems is an attempt to

- Understand the importance of Sangathamizh poems
- Revive the vibrant and dynamic values of Tamil culture and heritage
- Introduce it to the youth of modern world
- With the latest technology available at our hands.

Tamil

Tamil is a language with a literature that is classical— *i.e.,* it is ancient, it has an independent tradition that arose mostly on its own, not as an offshoot of another tradition, and has a large and extremely rich body of ancient literature.

The quality of classical Tamil literature is such that it is fit to stand ahead of the great literatures of Sanskrit, Greek,

Latin, Chinese, Persian and Arabic. The subtlety and profundity of its works, their varied scope, and their universality qualify Tamil to stand as one of the great classical traditions and literatures of the world. Tamil is one of the primary independent sources of modern Indian culture and tradition.

Sangathamizh Literature

Sangam literature refers to classical Tamil literature created between the years c. 600 BCE to 300 CE. This collection contains 2381 poems composed by 473 poets, some 102 of whom remain anonymous. Sangam literature is primarily secular dealing with everyday themes in a Tamil context. Much of the Tamil literature believed to have been composed in the Sangam period is lost to us, though detailed lists of works known to the 10th century compilers have survived.

The poems belonging to the Sangam literature were composed by Tamil poets, both men and women, from various professions and classes of society. These poems were later collected into various anthologies, edited, and with colophons added by anthologists and annotators around 1000 CE. Sangam Poems falls into two categories: the 'inner field' (Agam), and the 'outer field' (Puram) as described even in the first available Tamil grammar, the Tolkappiyam.

The 'inner field' topics refer to personal or human aspects, such as love and sexual relationships, and are dealt with in a metaphorical and abstract manner.

The 'outer field' topics discuss all other aspects of human experience such as heroism, valour, ethics, benevolence, philanthropy, social life, and customs. Sangathamizh illustrates the thematic classification scheme first described in the Tolkappiyam. The classification ties the emotions involved in agam poetry to a specific landscape. These landscapes are called thinai. These are: kurinji mountainous regions; mullai forests; marutham agricultural land; neithal coastal regions; paalai deserts. In addition to the landscape based thinais, kaikkiLai and perunthinai are used for unsolicited love and unsuited love respectively.

Similar thinais pertain to puram poems as well, though these categories are based on activity rather than landscape: vetchi, ‘karanthai, vanchi, kanchi, umignai, nochchi, thumbai, ‘vaagai, paataan, and pothuviyal.

Revival

Tamil, being one of the most ancient languages, yet vibrant and dynamic with its inexhaustible thoughts in every realm influencing humanity through its arts and literature has provided guidelines for happy living, just governance, noble behaviour etc. It's our duty to take this torch further in our time for the future by all the modern means.

The works of Sangam literature were lost and forgotten for several centuries. A revival took place from the late nineteenth century when works of religious and philosophical nature were written in a style that made it easier for the common people to enjoy. Several Tamil scholars such as S. V. Damodaram Pillai and U. V. Swaminatha Iyer. They painstakingly collected and catalogued numerous manuscripts in various stages of deterioration. They printed and published Tholkappiyam, Nachinarkiniyar urai (1895), Tholkappiyam Senavariyar urai, (1868), Manimekalai (1898), Cilappatikaram (1889), Pattupattu (1889), and Purananuru (1894), all with scholarly commentaries. Damodaram Pillai and Swaminatha Iyer published more 100 works in all, including minor poems. Nationalist poets like Bharathiyar and Bharathidasan began to utilize the power of poetry in influencing the masses.

With growth of literacy, Tamil prose began to blossom and mature. Short stories and novels began to appear. Many scholars including our Hon'ble CM have written books on sangathamizh poems. The popularity of Tamil Cinema has also provided opportunities for modern Tamil creative heads to take up sangathamizh in. Movies like Thiruvilayadal,

Mannadhimannan, Iruvar and so on, has references to sangam poems.

Why Sangathamizh Poems?

Sangam Poems are the authority for moral Life. They fall into two categories; Agam and Puram, referring to personal or human aspects, such as love and sexual relationships in the former and all other aspects of human experience such as heroism, valor, ethics, benevolence, philanthropy, social life, and customs in the latter. This cultural treasure is known only to Tamil scholars and is still out of reach of common mass.

This is because of lack of awareness of our heritage and culture and above all poor education. Though some of these poems are taught in schools and colleges, there is still no proper way to inspire the learner to have a further reading of the literatures.

Animated Sangathamizh Poems

Animated Sangathamizh Poems would be the adaptation of classical Tamil poems to modern music and animations without losing the values and traditional tastes. Poems from Ettuthogai, Pathu Paattu, Padhinenkeezhkanakku etc., are full of interesting scenes paving way for good visualisation of the glorious living of our Tamils. These poems can be visualised in animated format which will attract not only every Tamil, but also every human being in the globe who try to attain the ethical values.

How to Implement

Since the need of understanding cultural values in the society are increasing day by day, Animated Sangathamizh poems with musical rendering should reach the public through all the technological means available update. The challenge is quality, process and technology we are going to use so that it reaches the mass with a greater impact. The media in hand are Satellite channels, CDs, iphones and mobile phones. Since technology is improving day by day, High quality music, Stunning graphics and animations are possible to achieve the objective.

Music: Differing from the traditional way of composing music, the Animated Sangathamizh poems will have tunes to the taste of youth to attract them, at the same time without compromise in the relevance and values. Various music composers have proved that this is possible.

Animation: Stunning animations can be made for sangathamizh poems as they naturally have wonderful visuals and descriptive storyboards of past glory. Care will be taken to make the animations and graphic interesting, relevant to present day situations.

Meaning: The ultimate objective of the attempt is to reach this to the common mass. This can be achieved by using simple language for describing the meaning of the poems. People need not to literate to understand what is being said.

Advantages

- ***A great revolution***: This will be indeed a great revolution in revival of Sangam Literatures because through this attempt we can uplift the values of life which is found losing importance in the modern, fast world.
- ***Multimedia***: Throughout history, man has shown his fascination towards visualizing his creative thoughts in various available resources. The technologies available with us can attract audience of all stages of the social pyramid.
- ***Teaching/Learning aid:*** This can further be an excellent resource for researchers, teachers and learners where hours of time spent on by hearting text form can be reduced to a minimal time with permanent registry in mind.
- ***Future Generations***: This will certainly be a treasure for the generations to come as the world is becoming more and more modern and there is no time to turn back to even glance at the values which are missing.

Conclusion

In spite of being spoken by a whole race of people including the illiterate among us, Tamil has maintained such a continuity and uniformity that literature written 2000 years ago can be understood by the educated readers of the present. But we should not stop with this. Every common man, literate or illiterate should enjoy the essence of Tamil and we believe that Sangathamizh poems—being the most ancient literature, yet with inexhaustible thoughts in every realm influencing humanity through its words has provided guidelines for happy living, just governance, noble behaviour etc. It's our duty to take this further in our time for the future and one such way is Animated Sangathamizh Poems.

Representation of Kinship in WordNet

— S. Arulmozi

ABSTRACT

WordNet (Fellbaum,1998) is one of the most resourceful semantic lexicons in English. Its main advantage is that it is hand-crafted, so data stored within its semantic network are of high quality. It is used in most of the NLP applications, particularly in sense disambiguation tasks. WordNets are already available in most of the languages of the world including Hindi. Efforts are underway in Indian languages using the expansion approach with Hindi WordNet as the base. Kinship presents a tough problem in the construction of WordNet, especially in Tamil and other major Dravidian languages. This paper presents the lexicographical issues involved in the construction of synsets (synonym sets) in general and kinship hierarchy in particular. A brief account on the representation of kinship hierarchy in WordNet will also be provided.

Introduction

The Princeton English WordNet (Fellbaum, 1998) is one of the most resourceful semantic lexical database in English. Its main advantage is that it is hand-crafted, so data stored within its semantic network are of high quality. It is widely used as a resource in many NLP applications such as Information Retrieval, Word Sense Disambiguation, etc.

The continuous expansion of the multilingual information society with a growing number of new languages present on the Web has led in recent years to a pressing demand for multilingual applications.

To support such applications, multilingual language resources are needed, which however require a lot of human effort to be built. For this reason, the development of language independent resources which factorize what is common to many languages, and are possibly linked to the language-specific resources, could bring great advantages to the development of the multilingual resources in Indian languages.

Princeton's English WordNet inspired extensive development of WordNets in European languages, EuroWordNet (Vossen,) and also in other languages across the globe including WordNets in Indian languages, IndoWordNet (Pushpak). In this paper, a brief account on WordNet and construction of synsets is given. The paper is organized as follows: Section 2 details about WordNet and activities in Indian languages. Section 3 deals with the construction of synsets in general and pinpoints few problems faced during the construction of synsets.

Section 4 briefly lists the ontology of kinship in English WordNet followed by the problems faced in creating synsets for kinship concepts in Tamil and Telugu. The last section summarizes the work.

Word Net

WordNet was originally conceived and developed as a lexical

database for English on the basis of psycholinguistic properties. The major lexical categories such as nouns, verbs adjectives and adverbs are organized in terms of sets of synonyms (synsets) each representing a lexical concept.

A synset is a set of synonyms (word forms that have the same or similar meaning) and two words are said to be synonymous if their mutual substitution does not alter the truth-value of a given sentence in which they occur, in a given context. For example, {computer, computing machine, computing device, data processor, electronic computer, information processing system} form a synset because they can be used to refer to the same concept. These synsets are interconnected by certain relations, lexical relations such as synonymy, antonymy and semantic relations such as hyponymy (between specific and more general concepts) and meronymy (between parts and wholes).

An example of a synset is reproduced (from WordNet 2.1) here for clarity:

The synset for {computer, computing machine, computing device, data processor, electronic computer, information processing system} is related to:

— more general concept or the hypernym synset {machine}

— more specific concepts or hyponym synsets {analog computer}; {digital computer}; {node, client, guest}; {number cruncher}; {pari-mutuel machine, totalizer, totaliser, totalizator, totalisator} and {server, host}

— parts it is composed of {busbar, bus}; {cathode ray tube, CRT}; {central processing unit, CPU, processor, mainframe}: Each of these synsets is again related to other synsets as is illustrated for {machine} that is related to {device}, and {CPU} that is related to other parts {mother board, CPU board}, {circuit, electrical circuit}.

WordNet (2.1 version) has approximately 120,000 lexical items (word forms) organized into 100,000 meanings (word meanings). For most of the synset, a brief definition (gloss) is provided.

The success of the English WordNet has paved way for the emergence of several projects with the aim constructing WordNets in various languages and developing multilingual WordNets. EuroWordNet, a conglomeration of WordNets in European languages is an important project that has come up with a multilingual WordNets. Similar efforts are underway in Indian languages. Hindi WordNet is leading the way for all Indian language WordNets under IndoWordNet.

WordNet building activities in Dravidian languages started with the work of Tamil WordNet28 at AUKBC Research Centre using Rajendran's (2001) ontological classification of Tamil vocabulary. Work on Dravidian WordNet (comprising WordNets in four major Dravidian languages, *viz.* Kannada, Malayalam, Tamil and Telugu) started during a Workshop29 held at Chennai in which synsets were built for Construction Domain. Currently Dravidian WordNet30 activity is being carried out for Kannada at University of Hyderabad, Malayalam at Amrita Vishwa Vidyapeetham, Tamil at Tamil University and Telugu at Dravidian University.

Construction of Synsets

Various approaches are followed in the construction of WordNets across the languages of the world. For the Indian languages, WordNets are constructed using the expansion approach. For the construction of WordNet in Tamil and Telugu, we also follow the expansion approach,. *i.e.* Hindi WordNet synsets are taken as a starting point of departure. The concepts provided along with the Hindi synsets are first conceived and appropriate concepts in Telugu are manually provided by language experts. The Telugu synsets are then built based on the concepts created keeping in view the three principles, *viz.* Minimality, Coverage and Replaceability. Below we present the challenges/problems faced in the construction of core synsets in general and kinship synsets in particular.

Lexicographical Concerns

As mentioned earlier, Hindi concepts are first conceived and appropriate concepts are provided along with synsets in target languages. But during this process, problems occurred when we are faced with concepts that have no appropriate equivalents. For example,

Concept (HWN ID 7531): चालीस सेर की एक तौल
cAIIsa sera kI eka taula 'a measure of 40 kg'.

For this concept, there is no corresponding equivalent in Tamil or Telugu. But there are varying usages in different dialects. For instance, in Kuppam, the measure is equal to 10 kg whereas in Kadapa district of Andhra Pradesh it is 14 kg, whereas in Tamil Nadu it is 10 kg. When it comes to providing equivalent synsets, Hindi and Telugu and Tamil uses the same, *i.e.* maNu.

Concept (HWN ID 24): मादा शेर
mAdA Sera 'a female tiger'

For the above concept, there is no problem is assigning equivalent concepts and synsets, but when it comes to providing equivalent sentences (which we mostly translate for developing parallel corpora), we come across difficulty. In most cases, we do not use gender while providing translations. This is not the case with this concept alone, but in all the concepts involving gender. For example, female rat (HWN ID 335), female parrot (HWN ID 1278), etc.

Kinship in WordNet

In English WordNet, kinship is represented in the following way: Kinship is a kind of relatedness or connection by blood or marriage or adoption. It can be classified as: 1) **affinity or phylogenetic relation** which is in biology means a state of relationship between organisms or groups of organisms resulting in resemblance in structure or structural parts; 2) **descent, line of descent, lineage, filiation** which is the kinship relation between an individual and the individual's progenitors; 3) **affinity** which in anthropology is the kinship by marriage or adoption and not a blood relationship; 4) **consanguinity or blood kinship** which in anthropology is the kinship that is related by blood; 5**) parentage or birth** which is the kinship relation of an offspring to the parents; 6) **fatherhood** which is the kinship relation between an offspring and the father; 7) **motherhood** which is the kinship relation between an offspring and the mother; 8) **sisterhood** which is the kinship relation between a female offspring and the siblings; 9) **brotherhood** which is the kinship relation between a male offspring and the siblings; and 10) **marital relationship** which is the relationship between wife and husband.

When we come to WordNet building activities in Indian languages, Hindi WordNet which is the pioneer is taken as the source language for building WordNets. That is, Hindi WordNet's concepts are taken as a starting point and WordNets are getting built using the expansion approach. In the outset, this approach looks trivial and economical considering the interlinking of synsets of different languages. But when it comes to kinship relations, however, Hindi concepts create problems while assigning synsets in Dravidian languages, especially Tamil and Telugu. Let us examine a few in the following pages.

Problems in Creating Synsets involving Kinship Relations

In all, there are 54 concepts in Hindi WordNet which involve kinship relations. For the purpose of this paper, only the problematic concepts are taken into consideration which needs special attention.

1. HWNID 7379; भाई का लड़का/bhai ka ladka/'brother's son'

   Synsets : "भतीजा, भ्रातृज, भ्रातापुत्र, भतीजए अचतंस, अवतन्स" BatIjA, BrAtRuja, BrAtAputra, BrAtRuputra, BatIja, avataMsa, avatansa/

   When it comes to Tamil providing concept is a problem. Straightforward, one can assign . But when assigning synsets, one comes across ambiguity in the concept, *i.e.* which brother's son, whether one has to provide or or both. The problem is the same in Telugu too.

2. HWN ID 1804. भाई की लड़की/bhaiki ladkhi/'brother's daughter'

   Synsets: भतीजी, भ्रातृजा/BatIjI, BrAtRujA/

   This is similar to the one given in 1 above; whether one has to provide or both. The problem is the same in Telugu too.

3. HWNID 683: मामा की लड़की/mAmA kI la DakI/ 'uncle's daughter'

   Synsets: ममेरी बहन, ममेरी बहिन, मातुलेयी, ममेरी, भगिनी

   mammerI bahana mamerl bahina, mAtuleyI, mamerI BeginI

   The concept in Telugu can be given as/mAma kUturu/ But, when it comes to providing synsets, one faces the problem in elder-younger distinction. Because, in case of Telugu, if it is elder daughter then it is/vodhina/and younger is/maradalu.

4. HWNID 2861; मामा का लड़का/mAmA kA laDakA/ 'uncle's son'

   Synsets: ममेरा भाई, ममियाउत भाई, मातुलेय

   mamerA BAI, mamiyAuta BAI, mAtuleya

   The concept in Telugu can be given as/mAmA ko Dukku/. But, when it comes to providing synsets, one faces the problem in elder-younger distinction. Because, in case of Telugu, if it is elder son then it is/bAva/and younger is/bAvamaridi/.

5. HWNID 685: मामा का लड़का/PUPA kA laDakA/'aunt's son'

   Synsets: फुफेरा भाई, फुफेरा भईया, फुफेरा भैया, पितृष्वस्राय

   PuPer A, BAI, PuPerA BaiyA, PuPerA BaiyA, pitRuShvasrAya

   The concept in Telugu can be given as/atta koDukku/. But, when it comes to providing synsets, one faces the problem in elder-younger distinction. Because, in Telugu, if it is elder son then it is /bAva/and younger is/bAvamaridi/.

6. HWN ID 686: फुफा की लड़की/PUPA kI laDakI/'aunt's daughter'

   Synsets: फुफेरी बहन, फुफेरी बहिन, फुफेरी भगिनी

   PuPerI bahana PuPerIbahina PuPerI BaginI

   The concept in Telugu can be given as/atta kUturu/. But, when it comes to providing synsets, one faces the problem in elder-younger distinction. Because in Telugu, if it is elder daughter then it is/vodhina/and younger is/maradalu/.

7. HWN ID 9540: बुआ के पति या पिता के बहनोई/buA ke pati yA pitA ke bahanoI/

   the brother of your father or mother; the husband of your aunt'

   Synsets: फुफा/PUPA/

   This is an interesting concept in Hindi. In Hindi, the brother of one's father or mother as well as the husband of one's aunt is/PUPA/but when it comes to Dravidian language they are to be given as different concepts, *i.e.* 'the brother of one's father' as one concept; the brother of one's mother' as one concept and the husband of one's aunt' as separate concept. Let us detail these concepts.

(a) 'brother of one's father' is

(b) 'brother of one's mother is

(c) 'the husband of one's aunt' is

8. HWN ID 4673 पुत्री का भाई/patnIkA BAI/'wife's brother'

   Synsets: साला, सार, नकल करवाना, अश्रुर्य

   sAIA, sAra, nakalaparavAnA, SvaSurya
   The concept in Telugu can be given as/bAriya sOdaruDu/. But, when it comes to providing synsets, one faces the problem in elder-younger distinction. Because in Telugu, if it is elder brother then it is/bAva/ and younger is/bAvamaridi/.

9. HWN ID 6365: पति की बहन /pati kI bahana/'wife's sister'

   Synsets: ननद, ननदी, नदिनी, नन्दिनी, ननंद, ननन्द, ननदिनी

   nanada nanadI, naMdinI, nandinI, nanaMda, nananda, nanadinI
   The concept in Telugu can be given as/barta sOdari/. But, when it comes to providing synsets, one faces the problem in elder-younger distinction. Because, in Telugu, if it is elder sister then it is/vodhina/and younger is/maradalu/.

10. HWN ID 7194 वह जो संबंध के विचार से किसी के बहन का पुत्र हो

    /vaha jo saMbaMdha ke vicAra se kisI ke bahana kA putra ho/
    ... sister's son'

    Synsets: भानजा, भाजा, भान्जा, भागिनेय, बहनौता, बहनोत

    BAnajA, BAMjA, BAnjA, BA gineya, bahanautA, bahanota

In the above example, the Hindi concept is 'in relationship, it is anybody's sister's son'. But if one has to provide an appropriate concept in Telugu, then we have to split the concept into two. That is, if it is one's (male) sister's son, then the synset is/menalludu/and if it is one's (female) sister's son, then/kodukku/. This is the same in Tamil.

11. HWN ID 7195 संबंध के विचार से किसी के बहन की पुत्री या ननद की पुत्री

saMbaMdha ke vicAra se kisI ke bahana kI putrI yA nanada kI putrI

Synsets: भानजी, भाजी, भांजी, बहनौती, भगिनेया

BaAnjI, BA,MjI, BA~MjI, bahanautI, BAgineyA

The Hindi concept is more general, *i.e.* it does not make a distinction between the speaker, whereas when it comes to Telugu and Tamil, one has to make the distinction. If the speaker is a male, then his sister's daughter is, if it is a female, then her sister's daughter is.

In the above example, only few of the problems faced while constructing in Telugu and Tamil using Hindi concepts are presented. The reason for this is two-fold, *viz.* first, Hindi concepts are built based on most commonly used words, so one can see how shallow the synsets are and secondly, it is a problem of two different language families in the expansion approach. In Trauttman (1995) words, one needs a hierarchy of constructs, the genetic constructs – Dravidian and Indo-Aryan – and the synthesizing construct of Indian kinship to distinguish the Dravidian data from the non-Dravidian.

Conclusion

While WordNets are being developed for almost all the major Indian languages, one should give special attention while constructing synsets which is the core of WordNet. As seen from the examples above, it exemplifies that constructing WordNet based on Indo-Aryan languages into Dravidian languages is not a trivial task. It is also clear that kinship relation in Hindi WordNet is shallow and hence one has to take into account different culture specific constructs into consideration. This brings us to some interesting challenges in the construction of WordNets: How to integrate language independent constructs in IndoWordNet. How to handle problems such as male-female distinction in IndoWordNet and vice-versa; elder-younger, distinction which is prominent in Telugu but not in a cognate language such as Tamil?

How to represent kinship hierarchy in WordNet? The only solution at this point of time is to build a Domain Ontology within the framework of WordNet Domains.

REFERENCES

1. Cruse, D.A., 1986. *Lexical Semantics*, Cambridge: Cambridge University Press.
2. Fellbaum, C. 1998. WordNet: *An Electronic Lexical Database*. Cambridge: The MIT Press.
3. Forner, Pamela, 2005. WordNet Domains. ITC-irst, Povo-Trento, Itala, Document Version 1.0.
4. Kriyavin taRkaalat tamizh akarati, 2008. Chennai: CreA.
5. Luisa, B. *et.al.* 2004. *Revising the WordNet Domains Hierarchy: Semantics, Coverage and Balancing*. Coling 04.
6. Trautmann, Thomas R., 1995. *Dravidian Kinship*, New Delhi: Vistaar Publication.
7. Miller, G. A. 1990. 'WordNet: *An Online Lexical Database*'. Special Issue of International Journal of Lexicography, 3:4.
8. Miller, G.A. 1995. '*WordNet: A Lexical Database for English*', Communications of the ACM, 38: 11, 39-41.
9. Narayan, D., Chakrabarty D., Pandey P. and Bhattacharyya, P. 2002. '*An Experience in Building the Indo WordNet—a WordNet for Hindi*', International Conference on Global WordNet, Mysore.
10. Nida, E. A. 1975. *Compositional Analysis of Meaning*: An Introduction to Semantic Structure. Mouton: The Hague.

11. Rajendran, S. 2001. *taRkaalat tamizhc coRkaLanjciyam* [Modern Tamil Thesaurus]. Thanjavur: Tamil University Publication.
12. Tamil Lexicon. 1982. Madras: University of Madras Publication, Vols.1-6.
13. http://wordnet.princeton.edu/ (Princeton English WordNet).
14. http://www.cfilt.iitb.ac.in/wordnet/webhwn/wn.php (Hindi WordNet linked with Indian languages).
15. http://www.globalwordnet.org (Global WordNet Association).

Role of Regular Expression (RE) in Morphological Analysis

— *R. Shanmugam*

ABSTRACT

The aim of this article is to analyze the role of Regular Expression in Tamil Morphological Analysis. Morphological Analysis is essential for Natural Language Processing (NLP) and Machine Translation (MT). In morphological analysis, what we do is to parse the inflected word into root and affixes and then to tag them for grammatical categories. To build a Syntactic Parser, we need a Morphological Parser with POS (Parts-of-speech) tagger. The input for the Syntactic Parser is the output of the Morphological Parser. There are many formalisms and tools are used in the field of Morphological Analysis. Regular expression is one among the best tools for Morphological analysis.

Introduction

Regular expression is the standard notation for characterizing strings (combination of characters). It is a formula in a special language for specifying simple classes of strings. Formally it is an algebraic notation for characterizing strings. Regular expression was introduced by Kleene (1956). A string is any sequence of characters like letters, numbers, spaces, tabs, punctuation. Space which is also a character because it has encoding value. Regular expression needs a pattern (search type) to search strings. The following table shows how the words are matched by regular expression.

Regular Expression	Example pattern matched
/puththakam/	avaN puththakam patiththaaN
/kalvi/	kalvi aNaivarukkum avaciyam
/niir/	kutikka mir veeNntum

So the regular expression/puththakam/matches any string containing the substring puththakam like the above example. Here the slashes (around the pattern) are used to clarify what is regular expression and what is pattern. (This notation used in perl). The upcoming table shows some of the important Regular Expression symbols which are used in Tamil morphological parsing.

Patterns in Regular expression: (Based on Perl language)

RE symbol, Name	Example pattern	Match
/.. tint	marankkal ='/kaL/	Pattern matching symbol funds if 'kaL' is the substing of marankkaL
/( ), Open and	/marank (kaL/ai)/	Whether maronkkal or marankkglai
close parenthesis		
/|, pipe line	Sa = ~maramma. NithaN/	Whether Sa is maram or maNithaN
/?, Question mark	karuththuk?kaL	karuththkaL or karuththukkaL
/S, scalar	avarkaL =/kaLS/	Whether 'avarkaL' ended with kaL
-,	ceythaaN=~/th+/	One or more 'th' in ceythaaN
	patiththaaN = ~/th+/	One or more 'th' in patiththaaN

Levels in Morphological Analysis

There are three levels involved in Morphological Analysis such as 1.Root checking, 2. Affix Stripping, 3. Morphophonemic changes. We can use Regular Expression for the above three levels. It has much influence in Morphological Analysis. It is a very handy tool to make this kind of Morphological analysis. It can be implemented easily with Perl language.

The Role of Regular Expression in Root checking

This is a basic task in Morphological Analysis. Under this task, the root word existence in the database would be found. The following code may useful to know the importance of RE in this task.

```
open (filehandle, "C:\\DataBase\\Noun.text" \\die;
while (Sline = <filehandle>)
{
if(Sline = ~m^bSinput \b/)
{
$root word = $&;
last;
}
}
```

Here the line in bold is important. The character 'm' is stands for matching *i.e.*, to verify whether the database word is same with the end user input. '\b' is used to denote the word boundary. '$&' is called register in RE it is used to store the matched word into the variable $root word.

The Role of Regular Expression in Affix Stripping

Affix stripping is used to strip the affixes from the given input. The following sample coding explains the role of RE in Affix Stripping section.

Stripping tense suffix from the input stem "patithth"

```
if(Sinput = ~/([v|N|t|R])$| (pp?)$(iN)$|((n)?(th)+$|
(kk?in?R)S/)
```

```
{
Stense = $&;
Sroot = substr (Sinput, 0,-length (Stense));
}
```

The above code is having 14 tense forms for stripping purpose. It is a great strength of RE. We can implement this in one line and it gives the following output.

```
$input (Input variable) = patiththth
$tense = thth
$root = pati
```

The Role of Regular Expression in Morphophonemic Section

This section is playing the key role for this programming. This section includes three sub-functions such as addition, deletion, substitution. The three functions would be used to make the remaining stem into root. If we want to change the stem 'marathth' into maram the following code is needed.

```
$input = marathth
if(($input=~m/thth$/) and ($case ))
{
$input=~s/thth/m/;
}
```

Output: $input = maram

Here the bold lines are showing the importance of RE. 'if' condition is used to identify the occurrence of 'thth' in input and substitution is used to change the stem 'marathth' into root 'maram'.

Conclusion

Regular expression is a handy formalism to make Morphological Parser and it is common for languages we can adopt these ideas for other languages too, so that if we have a clear view on this we will make a good Morphological Analyzer for our language.

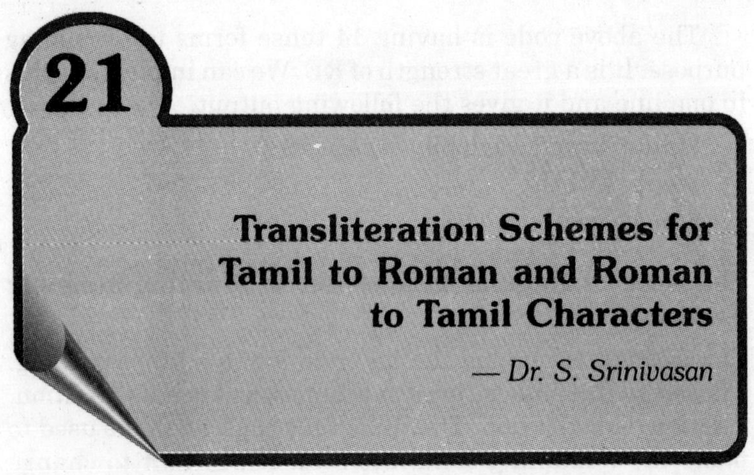

Transliteration Schemes for Tamil to Roman and Roman to Tamil Characters

— *Dr. S. Srinivasan*

Introduction

Here a machine transliteration scheme is proposed to map the random striking on a Tamil keyboard to Roman equivalent characters and vice versa. Many a language spoken in this world is associated with a native script. However a group of languages might also share a common script. For instance, the Roman script is shared by a number of European languages *viz.*, English, French, German, Italian and Spanish. If there is a means to spell out a foreign language using ones native script it lessens the burden of mastering another script and speeds up the process of learning. In such a situation, the transliteration scheme comes handy and helps to overcome the difficulty of knowing yet another script.

The Tamil Keyboard Layout

The mechanical Tamil typewriter consists of 4-tier structure and encompasses 23 consonants, 12 vowels, about 12 vowel modifiers, about 20 ukara vowel-consonants, one medial and a conjunct (Sri). Besides these the keyboard also contains shift key, dead key, caps lock and space bar. There are 4 schemes that are widely used for Tamil transliteration.

They are:

1. Madras University Tamil Lexicon Scheme—ISO 15919 Standard
   (Based on lower ASCII and a few diacritical markers)
2. Library of Congress scheme (based on lower ASCII)
   (a) It uses markers from upper ASCII block, *i.e.,* characters 128-255.
   (b) Variant of Library of Congress scheme (uses special characters such as # $ _)
3. University of Koeln-Institute of Indology and Tamil Studies scheme (based on lower ASCII, case sensitive and also uses digit 2)
4. ITRANS developed by Avinash Chopde (uses special characters such as ~ ^ besides other roman characters)

The objectives of the transliteration scheme are as follows:

1. The transliteration scheme could be case sensitive but shall not employ any special character or digit.
2. The transliteration must be unambiguous (loss less) and is primarily meant for machine automation.
3. The transliteration may not be ideally suited for human reading. Hence its user-friendly aspect is kept secondary.

Tamil-to-Roman Transliteration

Imagine an ape to snatch away a Tamil keyboard from a human hand and whimsically attempts to tap the keyboard to generate a sequence of characters. The strings of characters that are generated in the process may not be meaningful and some of them even contain a number of vowel modifiers occurring in succession (*e.g.* kombu,kaal, kombu...). To map such a sequence of modifiers, an improved rigid transliteration scheme is proposed. It is basically a variant of the UKoeln scheme.

None of the existing transliteration schemes are 100% romanized. All these schemes use either diacritical marker or special character or digit in addition to Roman letters. The UKoeln-IITS scheme uses the digit 2 to map the consonant Rannagaram and not any other special characters. Also this scheme does not differentiate between the pure vowel and its modifier. Hence attempt to improve upon this scheme was pursued.

The mapping for 'Rannagaram' was changed from n2 to nx so that the scheme becomes fully romanized. The choice for the letter x in lieu of 2 is the following.

nx => n(ExCHANGED) => 'tannagaram' exchanged to 'Rannagaram'

As the last bogie of a passenger train is indicated by the symbol X so also one can construe x to be the last consonant of archaic Tamil(y) and capital X to be the augmented last consonant of Grantha(OE) to the Tamil character set.

The word குர்ஆன் kurAn) was not properly transliterated from Tamil to Roman and then back to Tamil. Recasting the pure vowels from the vowel modifiers solved this problem. The vowel modifiers used in UKoeln-IITS scheme are:

a A i I u U e E ai o O au

To make the pure vowel representation unique the respective vowel modifiers were prefixed with capital

Y and the result is,

Ya YA Yi YI Yu YU Ye YE Yai Yo YO Yau.

The choice of the letter Y springs from the fact that the pure-vowel sounds close to the yakara vowelconsonant (uyirmey).

e.g.

ஆறு => யாறு; ஆனை => யானை; ஆண்டு => யாண்டு; ஆர் => யார்;
எமன் => யமன்; எந்திரம் => யந்திரம்; (பாந்தாமனார், அ.கி. 1955)
உரோனியம் => யுரோனியம்; ஊகம் => யூகம்; Yiddish => இட்டிஷ்;
Yield => ஈல்ட்; Yes => எஸ்; Yellow => எல்லோ

The prefixing of the letter Y for pure vowels may not appear weird if one compares the following transliterated words:

e.g. கடை =>kaTai ; கதை =>katai

Also in Tamil the pure vowels occur at the beginning of words. They seldom occur in the middle of words (aLapeTai is the exception). On the contrary the yakara vowel-consonants seldom occur at the beginning of words (yA is the exception). Case markers and words beginning with pure vowels when combine with a preceding Tamil word they change to yakara vowel-consonant.

e.g.

உடை/யணிந்து, இனிமை/யான, குடி/யிருப்பு, தலை/யீடு, உடை/யுடுத்து, உணர்ச்சி/யூட்டும், கை/யெழுத்து, இடை/யே, உதவி/யை, கை/யொப்பம், எத்தனை/யோ, நடக்கிறபடி/யால், மொழி/யில், அமைதி/யுடன், உதவி/யை, ஒலி/யோடு

Hence to differentiate between the pure vowel and its modifier the letter Y was chosen to be a part of the pure vowel. In English there are only two nasals (n and m). But in Tamil there are six nasals. Hence many of the nasals in Tamil need to be represented using more than one roman letter. Three of the nasal consonants (i i y) and a grantha consonant (‰) have to be represented by two Roman letters. In such cases the second letter (trailing part) was chosen to be unique and did not figure in any of the other consonant representations. If any phonetic semblance required its alternate case was chosen. The scheme employs 14 upper case letters of which 5 are used to represent the long vowels, one as prefix to pure vowels, 7 for consonants and one for conjunct vowel-consonant.

A I U E O, Y, N T R L J H X, S

The proposed transliteration table is given below.

க் ச் ட் த் ப் ற்

k c T t p R

ய் ர் ல் வ் ழ் ள்

y r l v z L

ங் ஞ் ண் ந் ம் ன்

ng nj N n m nx

ஸ் ஷ் ஜ் ஹ் க்ஷ்

s sh J H X

• ஸ்ரீ

q SRI

க கா கி கீ கு கூ கெ கே கை கொ கோ கௌ

ka kA ki kI ku kU ke kE kai ko kO kau

அ ஆ இ ஈ உ ஊ எ ஏ ஐ ஒ ஓ ஔ

Ya YA Yi YI Yu YU Ye YE Yai Yo YO Yau

A few of the problematic words are transliterated herewith.

e.g.

ஐந்து => Yaintu

அஇஅதிமுக =>YaYiYatimuka (a popular political party in Tamilnadu)

குர்ஆன் => kurYAnx(from kriya Tamil dictionary)

குரான் => kurAnx

ஆகா ! => YAkA !

ஆகாாா ! => YAkAAA

(one finds such usage in modern Tamil short stories- akin to emoticon usage in SMS and emails)

கை => kai

கைலாசம் => kailAcam

கஇலாசம் => kaYilAcam [பாறைப்புள்ளிக் கல்வெட்டு: கி.பி. 9-ஆம் நூற்றாண்டு]

(சிவலிங்கனார் அ. 1981)

தூது =>tUtu

துாது =>tuAtu (thinamalar Tamil newspaper uses this way)

|கெ =>eke [archaic Tamil usage]; |+| => ¨ (சம்பந்தன், மா.சு. 1981)

Also the split vowel modifier of aukaaram(ள) is construed as a combination of the modifiers kombu(|) and kaal(|): || =>eA; |+| => ள

Evidence to support this contemplation exists. (சிவசேகரம் சி. 1993)

The refinement of Tamil characters is also going on at slow pace. Reverend Veeramaa Munivar for the first time in modern era brought out orthographic refinement in Tamil. He devised a method to remove the ambiguity in the appearance of long and short vowels of ekaram and okaram about 250 years ago. The next refinement of Tamil characters initiated by the Tamilnadu Government and coinciding with the birth centenary year of Periyaar (E.V.Ramasamy) took place in the year 1979. To refine pure vowels with minimal change R.Krishnamurthy, the editor of Thinamalar Newspaper advocates the following modification for long vowels (கிருஷ்ணமூர்த்தி, இரா, 1978).

அ அi இ இi உ உi எ எi ஒ ஒi

Ya YaA Yi YiA Yu YuA Ye YeA Yo YoA

For instance Thinamalar newspaper recasts the Ukaarams œ, ß, à, à, æ, ê, ë to š¡, Ï¡, Ð¡, Ñ¡, Ö¡, Ü¡, Ü¡ and implements them in its edition. The aforesaid roman transliteration scheme is robust enough to take care of any foreseeable refinements in Tamil characters as well. The following is a sample text taken from Bharathidasan's work and whose transliteration is also given alongside.

அழுபவன் கோழை	Yazupavanx kOzai
ஆவின் பால் இனிது	YAvinx pAl Yinxitu
இரவினில் தூங்கு	Yiravinxil tUngku
ஈவது மகிழ்ச்சி	YIvatu makizcci
உள்ளதைப் பேசு	YuLLataip pEcu
ஊமைப்போல் இராதே	YUmaippOl YirAtE
எதையும் ஊன்றிப் பார்	Yetaiyum YUnxRip pAr
ஏசேல் எவரையும்	YEcEl Yevaraiyum
ஐந்திற் கலை பயில்	YaintiR kalai payil
ஒற்றுமை வெல்லும்	YoRRumai vellum
ஓரம்போ தெருவில்	YOrampO teruvil
ஔவை தமிழ்த்தாய்	Yauvai tamizttAy
கணக்கில் தேர்ச்சிகொள்	kaNakkil tErccikoL
சரியாய் எழுது	cariyAy Yezutu
தமிழ் உன் தாய்மொழி	tamiz Yun tAymozi

Roman-to-Tamil Transliteration

A rigid transliteration scheme is contemplated for Roman-to-Tamil conversion for the benefit of Tamils who can read only Tamil characters but wish to read English text as well. A parallel exists to this. Historically Tamils invented an alternate script to read Sanskrit text. It was called the Grantha. The Tamils preferred this script in lieu of the Devanagari script as it contained the Tamil alphabet too. In the same lines, an attempt has been made to map both the upper and lower case Roman letters (English characters) into Tamil.

Let us perform another thought type experiment. Imagine another ape belonging to North-Atlantic region to grab away a Roman keyboard from a human hand and strikes whimsically on the keyboard. Also assume that the digit and special character keys are disabled from the keyboard. In such a situation too, the string of characters that are generated may not appear meaningful and could even contain a large mix-up of both upper and lower case letters as nouns appear in German text. To map such a sequence of letters into Tamil a transliteration scheme is proposed. The contemplated case inclusive transliteration table is given below.

lower case								
a	b	c	d	e	f	g	h	i
அ	•ப	ச	ட	எ	•வ	•க	ஹ	இ
j	k	l	m	n	o	p	q	r
ஜ	க	ல	ம	ந	ஒ	ப	கு	ர
s	t	u	v	w	x	y	z	
ஸ	த	உ	வ	வு	க்ஷ	ய	•ஜ	

UPPER CASE								
A	B	C	D	E	F	G	H	I
ஆ	•ப்	ச்	ட்	ஏ	•வ்	•க்	ஹ்	ஈ
J	K	L	M	N	O	P	Q	R
ஜ்	க்	ல்	ம்	ந்	ஓ	ப்	கூ	ர்
S	T	U	V	W	X	Y	Z	
ஸ்	த்	ஊ	வ்	வூ	க்ஷ்	ய்	•ஜ்	

With the aid of the above table the following English words are transliterated into Tamil.

apple-	அபபலஎ	APPLE-	ஆப்ப்ல்ஏ
box-	•பஒக்ஷ	BOX-	•ப்ஓக்ஷ்
cat-	சஅத	CAT-	ச்ஆத்
dog-	டஒ•க	DOG-	ட்ஓ•க்
elephant-	எலஎபஹஅநத	ELEPHANT-	ஏல்ஏப்ஹ்ஆந்த்
fox-	•வஒக்ஷ	FOX-	•வ்ஓக்ஷ்
goat-	•கஒஅத	GOAT-	•க்ஓஆத்
horse-	ஹஒரஸஎ	HORSE-	ஹ்ஓர்ஸ்ஏ
ink-	இநக	INK-	ஈந்க்
jug-	ஜஉ•க	JUG-	ஜ்ஊ•க்
kite-	கஇதஎ	KITE-	க்ஈத்ஏ
lilly-	லஇலலய	LILLY-	ல்ஈல்ல்ய்
man-	மஅந	MAN-	ம்ஆந்
nose-	நஒஸஎ	NOSE-	ந்ஓஸ்ஏ
owl-	ஒவுல	OWL-	ஓவூல்
pig-	பஇ•க	PIG-	ப்ஈ•க்
quill-	குஉஇலல	QUILL-	கூஊஈல்ல்
rat-	ரஅத	RAT-	ர்ஆத்
snake-	ஸநஅகஎ	SNAKE-	ஸ்ந்ஆக்ஏ
turkey-	தஉரகஎய	TURKEY-	த்ஊர்க்ஏய்
umbrella-	உம•பரஎலலஅ	UMBRELLA-	ஊம்•ப்ர்ஏல்ல்ஆ
van-	வஅந	VAN-	வ்ஆந்
window-	வுஇநடஒவு	WINDOW-	வூஈந்ட்ஓவூ
xmas-	க்ஷமஅஸ	XMAS-	க்ஷ்ம்ஆஸ்
yacht-	யஅசஹத	YACHT-	ய்ஆச்ஹ்த்
zero-	•ஜஎரஒ	ZERO-	•ஜ்ஏர்ஓ

The reading of this transliteration may seem difficult in the initial phase. This situation is akin to asking a German to read English text or an English man to read German text. But this difficulty can be overcome in due course with adequate practice. The poet Bharathidasan himself felt that the alphabetical system of Tamil could be simplified if all the vowel consonants were split into pure vowels and consonants (பாரதிதாசன், 1948).

மறைவாக	நமக்குள்ளே	பழங்கதைகள்
(ம்அற்ஐவ்ஆக்அ	ந்அம்அக்க்உள்ள்ஏ	ப்அழ்அங்க்அத்ஐக்அள்)

சொல்வதிலோர்	மகிமை	இல்லை
(ச்ஒல்வ்அத்இல்ஓர்	ம்அக்இம்ஐ	இல்ல்ஐ)

He tried even writing so; but discontinued this effort in due course. In a nutshell the motive behind this scheme is the following:

1. To transliterate the lower case Roman letters into Tamil the following Tamil letters are used. They are short vowels, consonants, medial and a few ukara vowel-consonants.
2. To generate the mapping for the upper case Roman letters from the lower case Roman letters is simple.

They consist of either long vowels or pure consonants.

Applications

A random sequence of characters that are generated from a keyboard can be faithfully transliterated to another script and can also be used as a substitute for a password in computer applications. A password of this kind is all the more difficult to crack by a hacker. Transliterating a text to a non-native script and then encrypting it would add to the level of data security. The mapping from Tamil-to-Roman involves variable length and dual case and hence once encrypted it is difficult to decrypt. This feature enhances the data security in transmission as well as storage.

Conclusion

A machine transliteration scheme is proposed to map all the random sequence of characters that could be generated from a Tamil or a Roman keyboard. The transliterated characters could further be encrypted so as to increase the level of security.

Acknowledgements

The author expresses thanks to Dr.Vasu Renganathan, University of Pennsylvania, Philadelphia, USA and Dr. K. Kalyanasundaram, Lausanne, Switzerland for their help in providing the various romanized transliteration standards available for Tamil and offering valuable comments on this work.

REFERENCES

1. URL: http://homepage.ntlworld.com/stone-catend/translit.htm
2. URL: http://www.aczone.com/itrans/tamil/node5.html
3. பரந்தாமனார், அ.கி. 1955, நல்ல தமிழ் எழுத வேண்டுமா? சென்னை: பாரி நிலையம்.
4. சிவலிங்கனார் அ. 1981, தொல்காப்பியம் -எழுத்ததிகாரம் மொழி மரபு, சென்னை: உலகத் தமிழாராய்ச்சி நிறுவனம்.
5. சம்பந்தன், மா.க. 1981, எழுத்தும் அச்சும், சென்னை: தமிழர் பதிப்பகம்
6. சிவசேகரம் சி. 1993, தமிழும் அயலும், தேசிய கலை இலக்கியப் பேரவை, சென்னை: சூர்யா அச்சகம்.
7. கிருஷ்ணமூர்த்தி, இரா. 1978, தமிழ் எழுத்துச் சீர்திருத்தம். சென்னை: தினமலர் வெளியீடு.
8. Krishnamurthy, R. 1977, Script Reform in Tamil, Seminar on Socio Linguistics and Dialectology, March 27, Annamalai nagar: Annamalai University.
9. பாரதிதாசன், 1948, மே 15, குயில் திங்களிதழ், புதுவை.

22

From Classical Tamil to Computational Tamil

A Perspective

— Dr. A. Kumaran

ABSTRACT

The area of Computational Linguistics deals with computational models that are employed for analysis, synthesis or transformation of content in natural languages. Many well known end user technologies, such as, language understanding, machine translation, monolingual and crosslingual information retrieval and extraction, etc., are based on such models. Given the exponential growth of content in the Internet and Social Media primarily in vast majority of languages of the world, it is highly imperative that tools and technologies be developed to process the natural language data effectively and efficiently. In this paper, we highlight the state-of-the-art approaches for Computational Linguistics that are primarily based on statistical and machine learning principles, and underscore the need for clean large annotated corpora and language resources for any and all types of Computational Linguistics research. In particular, we emphasize the need for corpora, basic tools and resources in

> *Tamil, in order to ensure the development of technologies in the Tamil language. It is imperative that the community, academia, industry and the government come together to create a climate of consensus, coordination and collaboration to make sure that Tamil is taken successfully to the computational world.*

Introduction & Motivation

The area of Computational Linguistics deals with computational models for analysis and synthesis of natural languages, and is a vital predecessor for many natural language processing tasks, such as language understanding, summarization, information retrieval and extraction, machine translation, etc. Given the exponential growth of the amount of available natural languages data due to the Internet and Social Media, it is highly imperative that tools and technologies be developed to process the data effectively and efficiently. More importantly, in countries like India where only about 5% of the people are English literate, the need for such technologies is even more important for including the majority into the Information Age.

Computational Linguists research pertains to development of such tools and technologies. Traditionally, Computational Linguistics research and systems relied on linguistics research resulting in rules that are distilled by experts in a language. For examples, rules that govern morphological variations of a word or formation of a sentence in a given language are devised by experts, and coded into practical tools and systems. However, given that the natural languages evolve, such systems become unmanageable as they are fraught with relatively large portion of exceptions for every rule. Further, such rule-based approaches are expensive to create and maintain in terms of time and resources, as evidenced by decades of research put in the Western European (WE) and Chinese-Japanese-Korean (CJK) languages.

In the recent decade and a half, a host of newer approaches has been introduced in the Computational Linguistics Research, specifically; those based on Statistical and Machine Learning based methodologies. In these methodologies, specific tasks may be learnt automatically when provided with appropriate handcrafted training data. These methodologies are broadly referred to as statistical learning or machine learning algorithms. For example, identification of names or places in a sentence may be learnt (with a certain level of accuracy) by programmes that are trained on large hand-annotated corpora, so that they may be used subsequently for identification of names from sentences. While the quality of such depends on several factors: such as, the nature of the task, the algorithms used, features used for training, the quality and quantity of data used for training, etc., still such approaches had been proven to be very effective – as good or better than hand crafted systems for many of the natural language processing tasks. For example, all the state-of-the-art-translation systems in the world now are statistical learning systems.

In addition to being easier to develop, equally importantly, such methodologies are also largely language-independent, paving way for quick adaptation across languages. For example, a generic Statistical Machine Translation (SMT) system may be employed successfully to learn translations between any given pair of languages (with appropriate training data in those pair). Hence, such approaches exhibit a great advantage especially in countries like India, where a single system may be adopted for many languages, quickly and transparently. In essence, these methodologies rely on generic statistical and machine learning frameworks, trained on custom datasets.

Finally, given that the most popular medium for information, entertainment, commerce and governance – The Internet – is also turning multilingual31. The demographics of Internet users have changed from being predominantly

English, to more than two-thirds that are non-native English speakers now. In addition, majority of the information available over the web is in a language other than English. Such shifts in demographics suggest that the technologies must be developed for supporting predominantly multilingual user population, pointing to the critical need for language neutral Computational Linguistics research to cater to wider audience, quicker. In countries such as India, we face additional challenges where the population is mostly English illiterate32, hence tools and technologies in local languages are even more important, in order to overcome the digital divide to include the common man.

In the subsequent sections, we specify the type of corpora needed for Computational Linguistics research, and appeal to the Tamil linguistics and computational linguistics community to work toward common sets of standards and corpora to make the research community vibrant and fruitful.

Linguistic Corpora to be Developed

In this section, we outline several types of linguistic standards and corpora that need to be developed for Tamil, to support robust computational linguistics research.

National Efforts on Linguistic Corpora

National corpora are normally general reference corpora which are supposed to represent the national language of a country. They are collected by a consorted effort by the Government along with Academic and/or Industry players, in a focussed manner. These corpora are balanced with regard to genres and domains that typically represent the language under consideration, in that particular geographic or political domain. While many of the national corpora are available with parts of speech annotation, few of them have syntactic and semantic parses annotated.

The British National Corpus (BNC) is perhaps the first and best-known national corpus. It is designed to represent as wide a range of modern British English. This comprises approximately 100 million words of written texts (90%) and transcripts of speech (10%) in modern British English. In addition to Part of the Speech (POS) information, the BNC is annotated with rich metadata (*i.e.* contextual information). The American National Corpus (ANC) project was initiated in 1998 with the aim of building a corpus comparable to the BNC. The first release of the corpus contains 11.5 million words of written and spoken data. When completed ANC will contain a corpus of (100M) words comparable to BNC corpus. The corpus is POS tagged using different tag-sets to suit the needs of different users. Similarly there are national corpora available in Polish (130.8M), Czech (100M), Russian (100M), Hellenic (32M), German (100M), and Chinese (700M characters) languages.

In India, Central Institute of Indian Languages (CIIL) collected corpus is available in most Indian languages. However, this corpus is a relatively small corpus (approximately 3-8M words per language) primarily a monolingual text collection in multiple languages, with no annotation. While this corpus may provide the seed for data creation, the volume and quality of such corpus needs to be enhanced significantly, to aid Computational-Linguistics research in Indian languages.

Recently, Linguistic Data Consortium for Indian Languages (LDC-IL) has been initiated by the Ministry of Human Resource and Development under Government of India, to oversee the standardized collection of linguistic corpora in all Indian languages. Several academic and industrial partners are working together to get this collection created. Monolingual Corpora Monolingual corpora essentially refer to normal Tamil language text bulk from a standard source, such as, popular mass media, newspapers, television, etc. While it is good to have a wide variety of content; each genre, say, printed or spoken news, literary works, political speeches, religions writing, etc., each has its own characteristics, and best handled individually.

Ideally the text bulk should be in a standard encoding, such as Unicode, and annotated with some metadata, such as, source, author, date of publication, genre or category, etc. In addition to document level annotation, annotation of the content of the corpus itself could be extremely useful for many Computational Linguistics Tasks. For example, a corpus annotated with names (personal names, common names, places, dates, organizations, etc.), may be used for Named Entity identification tasks, and Information Extraction tasks.

Multilingual Corpora

Multilingual corpora refer to many types of corpora – parallel, comparable, etc. Parallel corpora are essentially sentence aligned corpus in multiple languages, where every aligned sentence pair contains the same semantic information in multiple languages. Such corpora may be readily used for developing Machine Translation systems.

In many practical situations, comparable corpora are more readily available than parallel corpora. Comparable corpora are defined as article aligned corpus in multiple languages, where the article generally is on the same topic, but may have different semantic content. Typical comparable corpora consist of news articles in multiple languages that cover the same news event; since each article may be written by different editor, it is likely to have similar, but not the same semantic content. Comparable corpora had been successfully employed in development of MT systems.

Annotated Corpora

Large annotated corpora are critically needed in any computational linguistics research. The annotation depends on the task at hand; for example, Part of Speech (POS) identification requires a rich annotation where every word in the text corpus is tagged, whereas Named Entity Recognition (NER) requires hand annotation of specific entities in the corpus.

Annotation Standards

Any type of annotated corpora underscores the need for annotation standards, in order to create standard annotated corpora that may be used by many tools and research groups consistently. It is imperative that standards be developed for annotation of the collected data such that the data created is rich enough to support many learning tasks that need to be based on the data, yet, flexible enough to be modified when the need arises. An example of such effort, is given in (Baskaran *et al.*, 2008), where a Part of Speech annotation framework – called IL-POST – was designed collaboratively by a set of academic and industry partners and which is applicable to a variety of Indian languages. Standard frameworks exist, such as EAGLE's (Leech *et al.*, 1996) for linguistic tagging.

Linguistic Resources

Many resources, such as dictionaries, thesauri, Bilingual or multilingual dictionaries are necessary for obvious reasons, for a variety of tasks. A computational dictionary must be in a standard format (Unicode, XML tagged) and must be machine-readable with standard tags. In addition, all references linking various words (for example, in thesauri) must be navigable using unique identifiers. There are specific requirements for computational dictionaries, as against print dictionaries.

Standards Organizations

Over the last few decades there are many very successful initiatives between governments, industry and academia in developing standards and corpora according to those standards. An example of such an initiative is the Linguistic Data Consortium (LDC) in the University of Pennsylvania.

Creation of Data with Community-wide Participation

It is important to highlight the importance of crowd-sourcing as a methodology for creation of linguistic corpora, as many types of corpora does not need to be created by linguists or language experts, but easily by the native speakers of a language. An initiative to generate parallel data is outlined in (Kumaran *et al.*, 2009).

The Need for Linguistic Corpora

In this paper, we focused on mining NE pairs in two different languages, namely English and an Indian language, Tamil. While we adopted a methodology similar to that in [Klementiev and Roth, 2006], our focus was on mining parallel NE transliteration pairs, leveraging the availability of comparable corpora and a well-trained linear classifier to identify transliteration pairs. We profiled the performance of our mining framework on several parameters, and presented the results. While the results show the potential of our approach, we also uncovered several issues that need to be resolved, for effective mining of parallel NE transliteration pairs. Given that the NE pairs are an important resource for several NLP tasks, we hope that such a methodology to mine the comparable corpora may be fruitful, as comparable corpora may be available in perpetuity in several of the world's languages.

REFERENCES

1. Baskaran, S., Bali, K., Bhattacharya, T., Bhattacharyya, P., Choudhury, M., Jha, G. N., Rajendran, S. 5., Saravanan, K., Sobha, L., and Subbarao, K. V. S. 2008. *A Common Parts-of-Speech Tagset Framework for Indian Languages*. In Proceedings of LREC 2008, Morocco.
2. Kumaran, A., Saravanan, K., Datha, N., Ashok, B. and Dendi, V. 2009. WikiBABEL: A Wiki-style Platform for Creation of Parallel Data. In Proceedings of ACL 2009.
3. Leech, G. and Wilson, A. 1996. *Recommendations for the Morphosyntactic Annotation of Corpora*. EAGLES Report EAG-TCWG-MAC/R.
4. Linguistic Data Consortium. http://ldc.upenn.edu/.

Spell Checker for Tamil using Finite State Automata

— *Anitha. S Pillai*

ABSTRACT

The problem of detecting and correcting misspelled words in text has received great attention due to its importance in several applications like text editing systems, optical character recognition systems, morphological analysis and tagging. Other applications like machine translation and information extraction, operate on text.There are possibilities that there may be errors in these text. The ability to automatically detect and correct spelling error should be of great help to those applications. The problem of detecting and correcting misspelled words in text is usually solved by checking whether a word already exists in the dictionary or not. If not, we try to extract words from the dictionary that are most similar to the word in question. This will not work for all languages where a large number of words can be derived from the root word and it is not feasible to store all the words in the dictionary. Hence a Morphological analyzer also plays an important role in these languages.

In this paper an approach for automatic correction of spelling mistakes in Tamil document using the Finite State Automata (FSA) is proposed.

Introduction to Spell Checking

This paper discusses the stages involved in the development of a Tamil Spell Checker. Since in Tamil, a large number of words can be derived from a root word, a purely dictionary based approach for Spell Checking is not practical. Hence a 'Rule cum Dictionary' based approach is followed. The lexicon (dictionary) is stored in the form of finite state automata.

The different modules in the Spell Checker Engine *viz.* Morphological Analyzer, Error detection and suggestion generation module are also explained. A Spell checker is a tool that will check the spelling of words in a document, validate them and in case the spell checker finds error, list out the correct spelling in the form of suggestions. Any word processor should have a spellchecker associated with it as the user may commit mistakes during typing. According to Damerau (1964), 80% of all misspelled words in a sample of human keypunched text were caused by single-error misspellings. It could be either due to insertion, deletion, substitution or transposition. Kukich (1992) breaks down human typing errors into two classes. Typographic errors are generally related to keyboard. Cognitive errors are caused by writers who don't know how to spell the word.

The spellchecker detects the mistakes and prompts the user with a set of suggestions, which will aid the correction of the misspelled word. The approach followed in the design of an Indian language Spell Checker has to be different from those for Roman scripts, because in Roman alphabet each letter is complete by itself and represents a sound where as in Indian languages the characters are more syllabic in nature and most of the consonants will have a vowel sound added to it. Unlike other languages, development of Spellcheckers for Indian languages, especially Dravidian languages like Malayalam, Tamil, Kannada and Telugu is a bit complicated. Here the suffixes, postpositions and case endings agglutinate with the verbs, nouns, adverbs or pronouns. Also one or more suffixes can co nbine with the base word. In other Indian languages, for *e.g.* Hindi, case ending will not agglutinate with the base form. Also combinations like verb-verb, noun-noun, verb-noun etc. are not permitted in many other Indian languages.

Hence Morphological analysis of the input word is a must for Tamil Spell checker. Tamil is a morphologically rich language in which most of the morphemes coordinate with the root words in the form of suffixes. Person, gender and number markings combine with the root words. For error detection and suggestion an efficient morphological analyzer is required. Spell checker application presents valid suggestions to the user based on each mistake they encounter in the user's document. The user either selects from the suggestions or choose to ignore the suggestions and accept the current word as correct.

Finite State Automaton

Automaton is represented as a directed graph: a finite set of vertices (nodes), together with a set of directed links between pairs of vertices called arcs. Each node corresponds to a state. States are represented as circles with name tags in them. Arcs are represented by arrows going from one state to another state. The final states are represented by double circles.

The machine starts at the initial state, runs through a sequence of states by computing a morpheme in each transition, and ends in the final state. The path moves from the initial point on the left to the final point on the right, proceeding in the direction of arrows. Once the arrow moves one step, there is no backward movement (Of course, recursion of an item can be shown by using closed loops). The resulting Finite State Automata (FSA) is deterministic in the sense that given an input symbol and a current state, a unique next state is determined. A deterministic finite state automaton (DFA) is perhaps the simplest type of machine that is still interesting to study.

However, it is an enormously useful practical abstraction because DFAs still retain sufficient flexibility to perform interesting tasks, yet the hardware requirements for building them are relatively minimal. DFAs are widely used in text editors for pattern matching, in compilers for lexical analysis, in web browsers for html parsing, and in operating systems for graphical user interfaces. They also serve as the control unit in many physical systems including: vending machines, elevators, automatic traffic signals, and computer microprocessors. They also play a key role in natural language processing and machine learning.

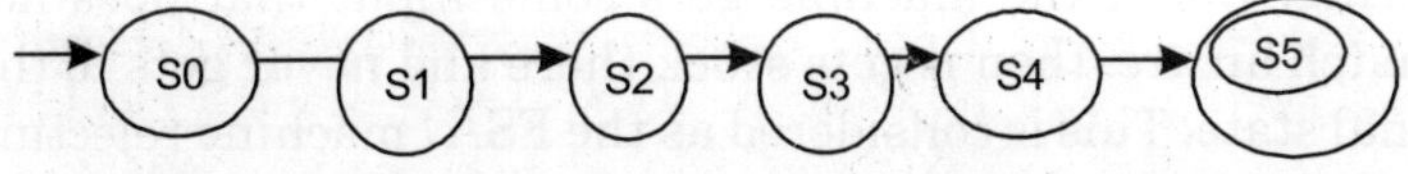

Structure of Finite State automaton

Here S0 represents initial state, S1,S2,S3 and S4 represents intermediate state and S5 represents final state. The automaton has five states which are represented by nodes in the graph. State S0 is the start state which we represent by the incoming arrow. State S5 is the final state or accepting state which we represent by the double circle.

Representation of words using Finite State Automaton

Tamil lexicon is stored as a Finite State Automaton. There is an initial state and final state for each word. The set of valid characters that help to move from the initial state to final state is specified for all the Tamil root words. *Eg*: initially the system is in state 1(initial state) when a character 'a' is input it goes to state2. From state2 on receiving the input 'm' it goes to state 3. The list of characters that characters that help 'a' to move from the initial state to final state is given.

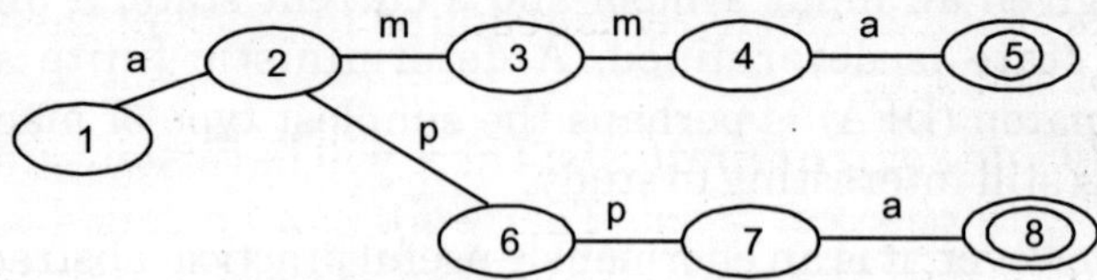

Representation of words amma and appa using FSA

Checking of Words

It starts at the initial state (S0), checks the next morpheme of the input. If it matches the symbol on an arc leaving the current state, then it crosses that arc, and moves to the next state, and thus, advances one symbol in the input. Such a process gets iterated until the machine reaches the final state, successfully recognizing all the morphemes in the input string. But if the machine gets some input that does not match an arc, then it gets stuck there and never gets to the final state. This is considered as the FSA / machine rejecting or failing to accept an input.

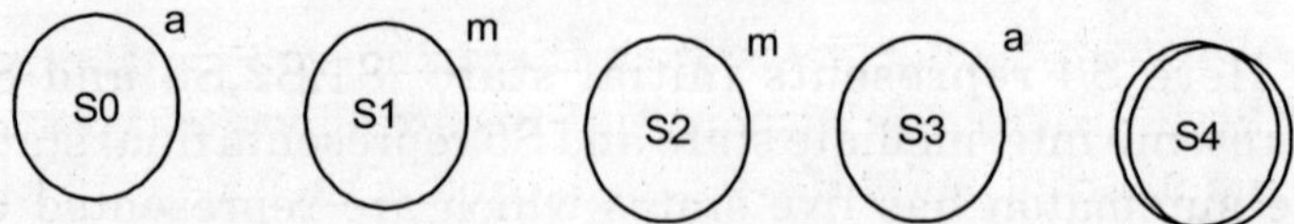

The word 'amma' is accepted by the finite state automata

Word not recognized by Finite State Automaton

If a set of input characters do not help to move from the initial state to final state then the automata will not be recognized for the given word. This could happen due to 2 reasons:

(1) The word is an inflected word *i.e.* suffixes are attached to the root word.

(2) Spelling mistake in the word

Inflected word : Root words to which suffixes are attached. These words will not be available in the lexicon. So Morphological analyzer is required to segment the word to root and suffix.

Morphological analysis: There will be certain suffixes along with the root word. This word can be called as an inflected word. The respective inflected word is stripped to its corresponding root word and suffix using backtracking algorithm such that the whole word can be written as root word+suffix. But in some cases when the suffix is stripped off the input string the root word will not be present in the root database. In such cases, we use orthographic rules which are solely used for certain words which are meant to be modified based on these rules.

For example: pasangal. In this word the 'gal' denotes the plural form. After the plural suffix is removed the rest of the word is checked with the root database. If the word is not present in the root database then orthographic rules are applied such that the input string is identified as correct.

Sandhi Checker

The Sandhi checker deals with the orthographic changes that occur in a root word when suffixes are added to it. When the input string has suffixes added to it and they are stripped off their respective suffixes, in some cases the root word may not be present in the root database. For example: consider the word 'pazhangal'. Once the suffix 'gal' is stripped off the rest of the word shows 'pazhang' which is not present in the root database. Here the sandhi checker helps in finding out whether the word is right or not. And finally the word is displayed as a correct word.

Suggestions

The minimum edit distance (or just edit distance) between two strings is the least number of elementary editing operations – insertions, deletions, and substitutions – that are needed in order to transform the first string into the second one.

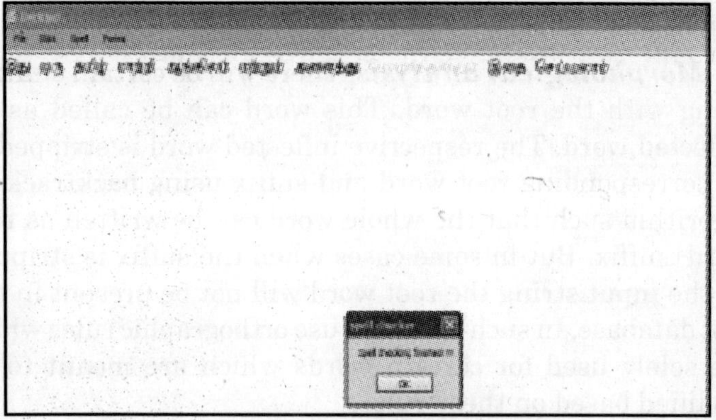

Screen Layout of Spell Checker

For example, the edit distance between the strings summer and summary is 2: we substitute the e for a, and then we insert y at the end. No other shorter edit sequence exists. Therefore, the edit distance is 2. These metric measures how similar to each other two strings are. Edit distance is also symmetric: if ed is a binary function mapping two strings to their edit distance, then, for every two strings s and t, ed(s, t) is always equal to ed(t, s).

The whole programme is developed using visual basic.net 2008 and MS-Access database. When the user types a word and if the word cannot be represented as a FSA an error is shown. This means that this particular word is not a correct one and so the FSA fails to move from the initial state to the final state. In such cases using minimum edit distance possible suggestions are displayed to the user to choose from. When the user types the word and press the space bar to type the next word, if there is an error then the word typed changes to blue. When the user right-click the mouse, suggestions are provided to correct the misspelled word. The suggestions are based on minimum edit distance.

Conclusion

Users can type text in Tamil and whenever the application encounters a misspelled word it highlights the error by changing the font colour of the wrong word to yellow. When we right click on this wrong word a list of possible suggestions are displayed.

REFERENCES

1. Thomas Lehmann (1993) "*A Grammar of Modern Tamil*", Second Edition, Pondicherry Institute of Linguistics and Culture.
2. Dr. K. Balasubramanian (2001), "*Studies in Tholkappiyam*", Annamalai University.
3. A Smart Spell Checker System http://www.coe.neu.edu/
4. Anandan. P, Ranjani Parthasarathy, Geetha T.V. (2001), Morphological Analyzer.
5. Tamil, ICON 2002, RCILTS-Tamil, Anna University, India.
6. D.Jurafsky and J.H.Martin "*Speech and Language Processing*", Prentice Hall 2000.
7. Yo-Sub Hana, Derick Woodb Obtaining Shorter Regular Expressions from Finite-state Automata Theoretical Computer Science 2006.

Automated Processing of Census Forms in Tamil

— *Shashi Kiran*
— *Rituraj*
— *Suresh Sundaram*
— *Swapnil Belhe*
— *AG Ramakrishnan*

ABSTRACT

This paper describes automatic form filling system for collecting census data based on online handwritten character recognition for Tamil. The aim is to facilitate easy digitization of Indian language ink-data gathered from field. The application interface is designed in such a way that the same application can be adopted for other Indian languages. It also describes the common interface framework required to facilitate this multiple language recognition engines. For Tamil or any other Indian scripts; inputting isolated symbols is not practical, hence the application uses non-isolated character recognition. The application incorporates simplified method of form design, layout analysis, engine error correction; engine level limited vocabulary based post-processor, validations etc. The performance evaluation of this application is also carried out against the traditional methods and promising results are obtained. The same system can be easily adopted for other types of forms required to be filled in Tamil e.g forms used by Government institutions, Banks etc.

Introduction

India is one of the very few countries in the world, which has the proud history of holding census every ten years uninterruptedly since 1872. The census provides information on size, distribution and socio-economic, demographic and other characteristics of the country's population. The data collected through the census are used for administration, planning and policy making as well as management and evaluation of various programmes by the government, NGOs, researchers, commercial and private enterprises, etc. [1]

Government agents visit each and every household in the country and collect complete data about the people and the condition of their houses. These agents gather this data by filling printed forms. The filled forms are then used to manually enter data in computers. This procedure takes long time and is prone to human errors while re-entering data manually. The data collection and the data storage are the two basic stages of this activity.

This census form processing system requires the members to carry the digital pads to the site, collect the information on this device, once the data collection is done plug in this digital pad to the computer and this application will generate the database. Gathering information by using printed forms is predominantly used in governmental, educational, banking domain. Even on-field surveys are carried out using local languages. Traditionally, the major surveys like census are conducted on field by pen & paper wherein a printed form is filled by a surveyor.

The surveyor collects information on the printed forms; and when the data collection is completed, forms are first scanned and then send for the verification and data entry. This method works well for small surveys requiring limited information. But when the survey requiring detailed information is to be carried out across cities, states and country; the traditional method becomes time consuming.

The large amount of time is spent on scanning, verification and data entry.

The goal of this automated census form filling system is to provide simplified form filling process which works with very low cost digitizers and considers major Indian languages. Reduction in cost of digitization is also considered during design of this system. In this system, the data collection process remains the same except an offline digitizing tablet is used for writing forms. The paper is kept on the tablet and the user writes on the paper by using special pen. The currently available offline digitizing tablets provide the advantage of retaining hard-copy of the filled forms for future use. These tablets with no display capture the ink data as X-Y co-ordinates and pen pressure. This collected ink data in X-Y co-ordinate format is then submitted to the form processing application which converts it to computer editable text.

Data Collection

The data collection phase is most crucial phase of the form processing application. The procedure for collecting data using digital tablet is similar to what currently being followed by data collectors. Instead of only-paper based forms the battery backed digital tablet is used along with digital ink based pen as shown below. The data collected on such digital device can then be downloaded on the Computer for further processing. This is where Tamil online handwritten engine come into effect.

The Surveyor who is collecting the data is required to follow the manifest for collecting data which is similar to traditional data collection. We have collected data from ten writers of Tamil for testing by using G-Note 7000 digitizing tablet working at 160 points/sec.

Architecture of System

This system is primarily divided into four modules for simplicity during development, the modules are,

- User Interface
- Input Data Extraction module
- Recognition Engine Interface module
- Database Generation module.

The application architecture is kept broad to easily plug-in different components. The application is currently designed to support two different types of digitizers namely Genius G-Note and iBall TakeNote but can easily be adopted to other devices. The Genius device produces the files with TOP extension while iBall produces files with DHW extension. As explained in the previous section the raw ink data (x, y co-ordinates) coming from the device is given to the application as input. Figure 24.1 explains the broad architecture of the application.

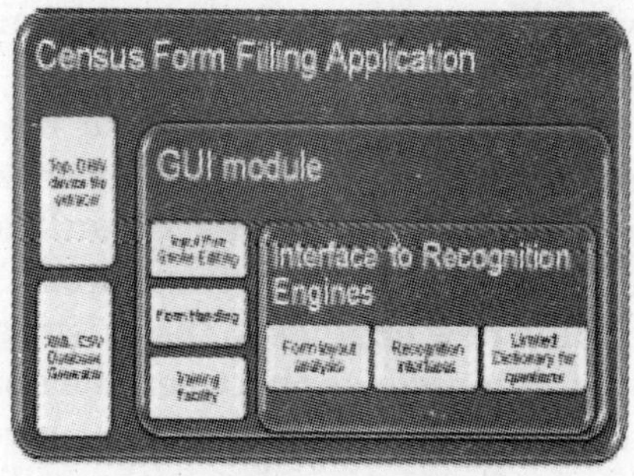

Fig. 24.1 : Architecture of Tamil Form Processing Application

The input data is displayed in full page format for verification. If the data contains any abnormal and misaligned ink strokes, they are removed by the operator. The verified data is then fed to the layout analysis module. This module aligns the input data to the pre-defined template using positional analysis.

This way, the answers by the client are mapped to corresponding questions. Once the correct alignment is achieved the text/numeral fields are separated from ticks. The text and numerals are given to Indic engines for recognition. This is achieved by using common interface framework used to link the Tamil handwritten recognition engine to the application. The output of the engine contains the recognized text with confidence scores. The confidence score is used to provide the operator with choice to select the correct outcome. If the score is high enough then no selection choice is provided. The operator is also provided with easy Tamil text editing functionality like virtual keyboard.

Common Interface Framework

Since this form processing system is designed to accommodate all Indian languages along with Tamil, there are many recognition engines to be interfaced to the system; hence there is a great need to have a standard communication protocol between different handwritten recognition engines and census application. A common Interface framework provides this vital link between the recognition engines and the application. This framework provides the flexibility to add/remove recognition engines. Also an entire new application can be built around this framework without the need of knowing the intricacies of online character recognition technologies. So this framework provides the scalability of adding new engines to the existing application. Simply put, it act as messenger between the application and the engine and thus helps to change any layer on the fly (*i.e.* we can change the application without disturbing the rest of setup or vice versa).

Pre-processing

Automated Segmentation

The segmentation of the validated data reduces the overhead of the Tamil recognition engine and helps in fast and accurate recognition of the handwritten text. All strokes in a page are given to segmentation module. In this module, all the strokes are arranges as per their position in a page irrespective of their order of occurrence. This module segments the lines based on horizontal projection of the strokes. Once the lines are segmented, the gaps between histogram (vertical projection) of each stroke on the line are clustered into within-word-gaps (WWG) and between-word-gaps (BWG) [2]. The words are separated by WWG.

Form Cleaning

The digital ink data collected by the surveyor often has noisy, unclean ink. Sometimes, the surveyor himself writes some notes, annotations, comments on the pages inside or outside the page boundaries. There also could be scrubbing which is large enough, crossing the full page or questions by digital ink. There could be overwriting, page misalignment or completely missing the pages of the form. This kind of data is required to be cleaned before proceeding for recognition. Otherwise the recognition accuracies could be very poor. Since it is difficult to clean all such noise automatically, the form cleaning is done semi-automatically. The cleaned, verified and segmented data is passed for recognition by the language specific engines.

Additional Features

Tick Detection

The forms used for census survey contains various data fields like text, numerals, check boxes etc. The surveyor is supposed to tick into the boxes wherever necessary. First, the check boxes needs to be separated from other fields. This is achieved by positional analysis of the form. Once the relative position of the ticks is identified, it is required to separate actual tick marks from the scrubbing and other unwanted strokes. The tick detection is used for detecting the check mark on the form; this includes fields like radio buttons or check boxes. There are various ways of recognizing ticks in this implementation we have used Dynamic Time Warping (DTW). It is an elastic matching algorithm for matching the similarity between two given sequences. The similarity matching is based on the distance measure. The sequence with minimal distance is considered for optimal match. Since the distance based sequence matching is not feasible for every point in sequences we need to put two conditions *i.e.* boundary and continuity condition. The continuity condition decides how much the matching is allowed to differ from linear matching [3, 4]. The Boundary condition states that first and last points of sequences will be matched with each other. The continuity condition decides the measure of elasticity given by the formula:

$$\frac{N_2}{N_1}i - cN_2 \leq j \leq \frac{N_2}{N_1}i + cN_2$$

Where c is the continuity constant, N1 and N2 are the number of points in first and second curve respectively. The points i and j of the first and second curve respectively can be matched only if above condition is satisfied. For c=0 the resulting match is same as linear matching.

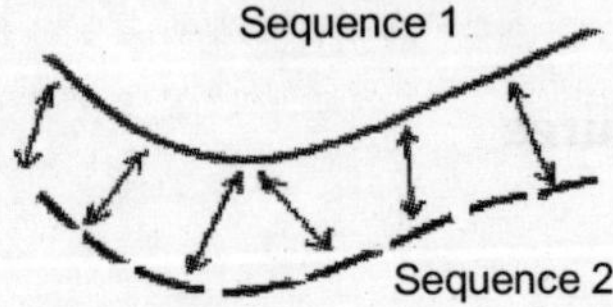

Fig. 24.2 : DTW matching of two ticks

DTW is trained on data collected from 20 clients, for ten different styles of writing ticks. Certain conditions are applied to the data before passing the data to DTW such as checking for number of strokes.

Error Correction Measures

The recognition accuracy of the underlying Tamil handwritten recognizer is not 100% hence it becomes responsibility of the application developer to highlight those inaccuracies to the operator in a mild way. The ideal application for such kind of systems would be one which not only gives the operator the helping hand in case of a recognition error but also trains the engine over time by understanding corrections made by operator. It also allows editing the input file with stroke addition/deletion functionality and saving the same.

Significant percentages of operators are bound to get irritated in case of repeated errors on part of recognition (governed by recognition engines). An effective user interface in this case would be able to minimize the edits required by use of automatic focusing, multimodal inputting, easy suggestion list etc.

The application is built with stroke correction facility. If the ink data contains spelling mistakes or ambiguities then the operator can re-write the strokes and save it for future use. The operator is also given the facility to type using virtual keyboards. The complete application is localized for Tamil. Since each field is separated by the values it may have, like text, numerals, numerals with symbols etc.

The application performs the broad validity check on each output returned by the engine. This helps in narrowing down the errors for each field. Based on the probability measure returned by the Tamil recognizer engine, the application takes the decision on whether the recognized text is suitable for displaying. If not, the field is marked with red colour pointing to the operator about possible error that may require relook.

Standardized Output Format

The operator is given the flexibility to save the recognized data in Unicode based Comma Separated Variable (CSV) files or Extended Mark-up (XML) files. These files can be easily imported by any of the database engines like Oracle, SQL etc.

Wordlist for Post-Processing

The common interface framework includes the interface to send the domain specific Tamil wordlists to the handwritten recognizer. The application developer changes the wordlists as per different requirements of the applications and sends it to engines so that language models can be applied in order to improve the performance. The structure of the wordlist is defined by the framework.

Results and Discussions

We compared the performance of this automated census form filling application with the traditional ways of conducting census surveys. The performance of the application is highly dependent on the recognition accuracy of the Tamil Online handwritten recognizer. Application uses some domain specific knowhow of census form data to improve on the base recognizer performance. In the traditional surveys, the filled forms are scanned and then manual data entry is done. In this experiment the census form used for evaluation was very comprehensive spanning over 10 pages. Following table shows the composition of the form used for the survey.

Field Type	Number of fields per form
Text (with wordlist)	8
Text (without wordlist)	17
Numerals	22
Check boxes (multiple ticks)	10
Radio boxes (single ticks)	27

The text fields like clients education background, spoken language, city, district, state etc. were backed with limited dictionary while fields like name, last name, address etc. were without dictionary. For evaluating performance of traditional census data entry, the forms were given to 3 data entry operators who were regulars in Tamil typing. Total data was collected from 10 writers; each form contained 10 pages. The same forms are processed through this application. Following table shows the comparative results of traditional manual data entry and online character recognition based application.

	Average Time (Time/Form) (10 pages per form)	Average Error in output
Manual Data Entry	89.09 sec.	2.68%
Automated Form processing + Verification	30.37 sec.	13.88%

As seen from the above table, the manual data entry took more time but numbers of errors were less. Note that the page scanning time required for manual data entry is not considered in the above table.

Conclusion & Future Work

In our experiment, the online handwritten character recognition based form processing for Tamil clearly showed a promising area for further research especially where collecting huge quantities of data from field and converting it into editable text is concerned. In this application we retain the paper based form filling & editing thus allowing more natural text inputting and reduce cost incurred on display based inputting devices. In future, we would like to study the impact of the Indian language word models on user acceptance of online handwriting recognition.

Acknowledgment

The authors would like to thank Consortium for "Online Handwritten Character Recognition" and Technology Development for Indian Languages (TDIL), Department of Information Technology (DIT), Government of India for funding this consortium project. The authors would also like to thank all the consortium chief investigators and members consisting of IISc-Bangalore, ISI-Kolkata, IIT-Madras, IIIT-Hyderabad, CDAC-Pune for their valuable inputs.

REFERENCES

1. Ashish Krishna, Girish Prabhu, Kalika Bali, Sriganesh Madhvanath, *Indic Scripts based Online form Filling—A Usability Exploration*, 11th International Conference on Human-Computer Interaction (HCI), Las Vegas, 2005.
2. Soo H. Kim, S. Jeong, Guee-Sang Lee, Ching Y. Suen, *Word Segmentation in Handwritten Korean Text Lines Based on Gap Clustering Techniques*, Proceedings of the Sixth International Conference on Document Analysis and Recognition (ICDAR-'01), Seattle, WA, pp. 189-193.
3. Ralph, Niels and Louis, Vuurpijl, *Dynamic Time Warping Applied to Tamil Character Recognition*, Proceedings of Eight International Conference on Document Analysis and Recognition (ICDAR'05), pp. 730-734.
4. N. Joshi, G. Sita, A. G. Ramakrishnan, and S. Madhvanath, *Comparison of Elastic Matching Algorithms for Online Tamil Handwritten Character Recognition*, Proceedings of the Ninth International Workshop on Frontiers of Handwritten Recognition (IWFHR'04), pp. 444–449.
5. XStroke: Full-screen Gesture Recognition for X, Carl D.—Worth Information Sciences Institute University of Southern California Arlington.
6. UPX—The best from UNIPEN and ink ML, - http://unipen.nici.kun.nl/upx/, 2002.
7. Swapnil Belhe, Srinivasa Chakravarthy, A.G. Ramakrishanan, *XML Standard for Indic Handwritten Indic Database* Proceedings of International Workshop on Multilingual OCR (MOCR-09), Barcelona, Spain, July 2009.

25

Pattern based English Tamil Machine Translation

— *S. Saravanan*
— *Dr. A.G. Menon*
— *Dr. K. Soman*

Introduction

The native languages all over the world are growing rapidly along with the growth of technology, in general, and information technology, in particular. On the one hand the world experiences a growth in the native language and on the other hand precious and nascent information come through foreign languages. Literacy in the mother tongue is no longer enough to follow the information supplied by the other languages. Because of this ever increasing gap and the speed with which information are supplied, it is necessary to bridge this gap with the help of modern technologies as early as possible. It is in this context that we are working on a Machine Translation (MT) system. Even though, there are several approaches to develop a MT system, LTAG-based MT and SMT are very prominent. SMT is far away from tasting the success in case of agglutinative languages like Tamil. The only available MT system for

English-Tamil is LTAG-based developed by AMRITA in collaboration with CDAC, funded by DIT. Transfer rules in LTAG-based MT are a pair of trees. Writing a new transfer rule is not very easy.

This paper proposes the use of pattern-based reordering rules in MT. Unlike the translation patterns in pattern-based CFG for MT (Koichi Takeda), the pattern based reordering rules are not lexicalized and the features and agreements are not handled in the rule. The source rules of these reordering rules are not used for parsing the source sentence. These rules are used to reorder the source phrasal structure to get the target phrasal structure. The English words are translated and lexicalized separately and this process is called lexicalization. The features and agreements are collected from the parse tree and used for synthesizing the words.

Parsing

One of the first steps is the identification of the structure with a parsing algorithm. Different parsing algorithms are available for the syntactic analysis of the source sentences. We are using the Stanford PCFG parser for the analysis of the source sentences in English. The sample parse output of the English sentence "Ram gave him a book" is shown in the Figure 25.2.

Pattern based Reordering

A pattern is a pair of CFG rules (Takeda, Koichi: 1996). These rules give the equivalent structures in the source and target languages. On the basis of the patterns the reordering rules are formulated to facilitate the machine translation. They reflect the translation patterns of the source and target languages. For example, the following reordering rule is based on an English—Tamil pattern: VP (VBD NP NP) _ VP (NP NP VBD) | | 1:2 2:3 3:1.

'VP (VBD NP NP)' is the English CFG rule ('VP' is the root node and 'VBD', 'NP', 'NP' are the children nodes in the tree representation) called a source rule and 'VP (NP NP VBD)' is the Tamil CFG rule called a target rule. "1:2 2:3 3:1" is the transfer link. The tree representation of the above rule is shown in the Figure 25.1 below.

Fig. 25.1 : Recording Rule.

The transfer link contains the order of the children nodes of the target rule. "1:2 2:3 3:1" says first child of the target rule is from second child of the source rule; second child of the target rule is from third child of the source rule, so on and so forth. The parse tree of the source language is checked against the source rules. If any match is found in the parse tree, then the source rule is replaced with the corresponding target rule. For example, the parse tree of the English sentence, "Ram gave him a book" is (S (NP (NNP Ram)) (VP (VBD gave) (NP (PRP him)) (NP (DT a) (NN book)))). This English phrasal structure is checked with the available reordering rules for finding a match. The pattern in the source language such as 'VP (VBD NP NP)' is present in the English phrasal structure and it is eligible for undergoing the reordering rule. The pattern "VP (VBD NP NP)" of the source language is thus replaced with its counterpart "VP (NP NP VBD)" in the target language.

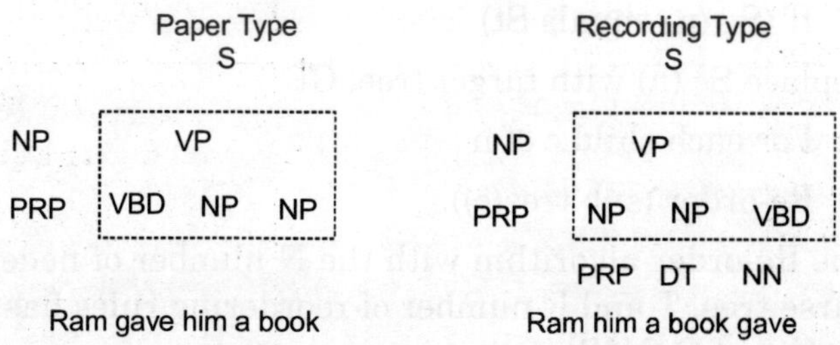

Fig. 25.2 : Transformation of Paper Type to Recording Type

Tamil shows a very high degree of flexibility in ordering the words within a sentence. The position of the words can be easily transposed without much change in the meaning. For example, "Ram gave him a book" can be reordered in multiple ways in Tamil, and the most common ways are: Ram him a book gave, Ram a book him gave, Him a book Ram gave, etc. The predicate verb takes mostly the last position.

In our system, the reordering rules are strictly one to one map. Every source rule is mapped to one target rule. Based on the most common usage, the target rule is formulated. The Tamil clausal structure is more rigid and shows little flexibility. For example, "Ram, who is smart, gave him a book." is reordered as "(smart Ram) (him) (a book) (gave)". Here the adjectival clause 'who is smart' has to be positioned before the noun 'Ram' in Tamil.

Reordering Algorithm

Let T be the parse tree with N number of nodes that we process for reordering; R be the number of reordering rules; St be the source rule tree; Gt be the target rule tree; Sc (n) be the sub tree of the node, n with the depth one. For example, the Sc (VP) in the parser tree is VP (VBD NP NP).

Re-order (T)

Visit node n

If n equals root (St)

For each St of reordering rule R

If (Sc (n) equals St)

Replace Sc (n) with target tree, Gt

For each child c of n

Re-order (sub tree(c)).

The Re-order algorithm with the N number of nodes in the parse tree, T and R number of reordering rules has the complexity of O (N*R).

Lexicalization

The words in the terminal node of the reordered tree are lemmatized and the equivalent of that lemma in target language is replaced in the terminal node of the reordered tree. For example, lemma of the source word 'gave' is 'give' and its equivalent in target language is 'koTu'. The target equivalents are found in the root word lexicon which contains the root forms of the source words and target words along with the POS category.

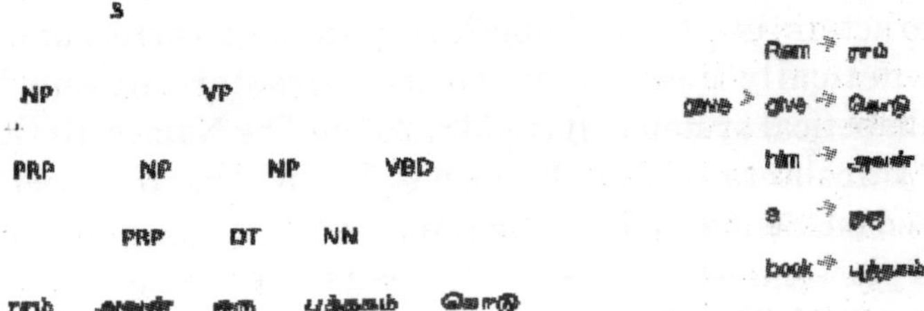

Fig. 25.3. Lexicalise Tree **Fig. 25.4. Laxicant**

The major challenge in the lexicalization process is semantics. There would be multiple senses for the source word. In that case, the current system has the provision for multiple outputs. In the case of the functional words and auxiliary words, there are no direct equivalents in Tamil. For example, "The auditorium is decorated for the college day celebrations", the words 'for' and 'the' do not have equivalent words in Tamil. 'for' comes as a post position (kkAka) in Tamil and is synthesized along with the Noun 'college-day'. The auxiliary word 'is' has no direct equivalent in Tamil. The words 'college day' consists of two entities in source and the equivalents for these two words separately are 'kallUri nAL' which is semantically wrong. The compound nouns are to be considered as one entity. The equivalents of the words 'college-day' as single entity are 'kallUri ANTu vizha'. The compound nouns are found and marked as single entity using the POS of the source sentence. The POS of this example sentence is, "The/DT auditorium/NN is/VBZ decorated/VBN for/IN the/DT college/NN day/NN celebrations/NNS".

Here the words 'college' and 'day' are annotated as 'NN'. The consecutive words that annotated as 'NN' are marked as single entity in the pre-processing, and during lexicalization the equivalents of this entity are found and replaced in the terminal node.

Transliteration

Transliteration is an automatic method that converts words/characters in one alphabetical system to corresponding phonetically equivalent words/characters in another alphabetical system(Vijaya MS, 2009). The Named-Entities are transliterated from English to Tamil using the tool that based on 'Sequence Labelling Approach'. 30k person names and place names (English-Tamil pairs) are used for training using SVM. The words that are not present in the root lexicon (Out Of Vocabulary words) are also transliterated in the same manner.

Synthesizer

The Morphological synthesizer glues the lemma and the morphemes to form a word using orthographic and morphophonemic rules. The lite version of Amrita Morphological Analyzer and Generator (AMAG) is used for synthesizing the words. The synthesizer requires the information along with lemma as an input. This information has to be gathered from the lexicalized target phrasal structure, the parse tree of the source and from the typed dependency information. The lexicalized tree has the lemma of the target language in the terminal nodes. Synthesizing these lemmas is very important in the process of translation. Synthesizing the noun gives the relationship between two nouns and in the case of verb it glues the TAM and gender information with the verb.

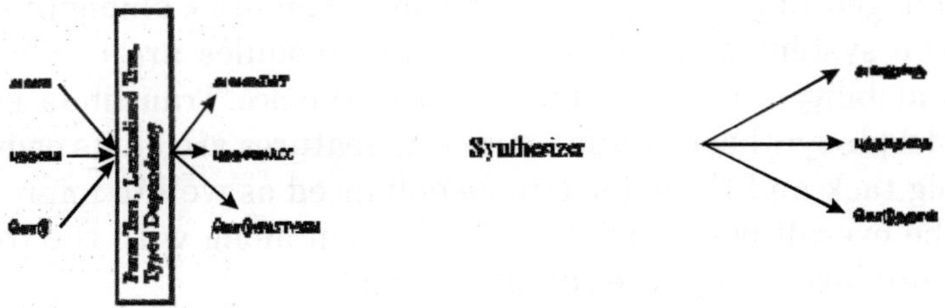

Fig. 25.5 : Synthesizer

For example, the word 'avan' is given as input to the synthesizer with the morpheme information 'DAT' as 'avan + DAT' (dative). The first level of the synthesizer replaces the morpheme information with the correct morpheme that to be synthesized with the lemma as 'avan + ku'. The second level of the synthesizer applies the spelling rule on 'avan + ku' and after the application of all possible rules; the second level outputs the synthesized word 'avanukku'.

Testing and Results

The current system is tested with the corpora of Tourism domain that we developed for DIT funded EIL, MT project. On testing with the corpora of the size of 2000 sentences, 60% of the sentences are translated well and 70% of the sentences are comprehendible. On the module wise testing, 80% of the sentences are reordered perfectly, 60% of the sentences are lexicalized properly with its correct target word, and the accuracy of the transliteration module is 93.3% and more than 90% of words that process through synthesizer module are synthesized properly, provided the information extracted and given as input to the synthesizer module is correct.

Conclusion

At present, the prototype version of the MT is developed with the 20k lexical entries and very few (40) reordering rules. In future, Word-Sense-Disambiguation-module can be plugged-in to the system to resolve semantics ambiguities. The system with all the necessary modules are in place, scalability is a key to improve its performance. Transliteration, Morph-synthesizer and extracting features are on its own a big task and these have to be enhanced as well to improve the overall performance of the system along with the root word lexicon and the reordering rules.

REFERENCES

1. Abeilld, A., Schabes, Y. and Joshi, A.K. 1990. *Using Lexicalized tags for Machine translation*. Proceedings of the 13th International Conference on Comparative Lingusitics, August 1990, Vol. 3: 1-6.
2. Menon, A.G. Saravanan S, Loganathan R, Soman, K.P. 2009. *Amrita Morph Analyzer and Generator for Tamil: A Rule Based Approach*. 8th Tamil Internet Conference, October 2009: 239-243.
3. Nagao, M., Tsujii, J. and Nakamura, J. 1985. *The Japanese Government Project of Machine Translation*, Computational Linguistics 11 (2-3): 91-110.
4. Nirenberg, S. (Ed.) 1987. *Machine Translation – Theoretical and Methodological Issues*, Cambridge: Cambridge University Press.
5. Rambow, O. and Satta S. 1996. *Synchronous Models of Language*, Proceedings of the 34th *Conference of ACL*, June 1996: 116-123.
6. Sato S. and Nagao, M. 1990. *Toward Memory-based Translation*, Proceedings of the 13th *Conference of COLING*, August 1990, Vol.3: 247-252.
7. Shieber, S.M. and Schabes Y. 1990. *Synchronous Tree-Adjoining Grammars*, Proceedings of the 13th Conference of COLING, August 1990: 253-258.
8. Sumaja Sasidharan, Loganathan R. and Soman K.P. 2009. "*English to Malayalam Transliteration Using Sequence Labelling Approach*", International Journal of Recent Trends in Engineering, May 2009: Vol 1, No. 2.
9. Takeda, K. 1996. *Pattern-Based Context-Free Grammars for Machine Translation*, Proceedings of the 34th Conference of ACL, June 1996: 144-151.

Bilingual TTS for Tamil and English

— AG Ramakrishnan
— Vikram L.R.
— Abhinava
— Shiva Kumar H.R.

ABSTRACT

An unlimited vocabulary text-to-speech engine has been developed, which currently handles both Tamil and Kannada Unicode text. The input text is processed by a grapheme to phoneme converter module, which uses language specific pronunciation rules to convert the text into an unambiguous phonetic representation. This text is then parsed into demisyllable like basic units. The occurrence of these basic units are searched for, from the phonetically rich spoken database, which is segmented and annotated at the phone level. An unit selection algorithm then selects the best combination of the available speech units to be concatenated to synthesize the speech, which is then converted into .wav format.

Introduction

Text to Speech (TTS) synthesis is an automated encoding

process, which converts the given text in a specific language into speech. Till date, only English and some European language TTS systems have gained commercial importance due to their quality output. This paper primarily deals with developing a modular, unit selection based TTS framework for Indian languages. Bilingual Tamil and English TTS is developed for this purpose. However, this framework can be easily modified for any other language. The TTS framework developed is concatenation based, with polyphone taken as the unit of concatenation. This framework is further optimized to suit embedded applications like mobiles and PDAs.

We designed and developed corpus-based concatenative Tamil speech synthesizer in Matlab and C. A concatenation based speech synthesizer requires a rich and large speech database with varied and natural distribution of prosodic and spectral characteristics of speech sounds. The sentences to be recorded need to be selected from a text corpus. We used CIIL (Central Institute of Indian Languages, Mysore) Tamil text corpus for our research. A greedy algorithm is used to select phonetically rich sentences from this huge corpus. This resulted in 1026 sentences, which were recorded from a professional, native Tamil speaker. These sentences are segmented offline and the database is organized in such a way that it facilitates faster search.

During synthesis, from the phonetic transcription of the sentence to be synthesized, specifications of the required target units are predicted. Units are then selected from the database that best match the target specification according to a distance metric and a concatenation quality metric. These units are then concatenated to produce synthetic speech. There may be audible glitches in the output after concatenation. This could be because of either poor segmentation of the speech database or improper selection of units by the TTS frame work. In our case, we know that the segmentation is nearly error-free. Hence, post-processing is performed on the final set of units. This includes smoothing the pitch contour, during concatenation, at junctions of units with unacceptable pitch discontinuity. Our experiments reveal that about 15-20% of the unit junctions require pitch smoothing. Optimal coupling technique is then used to concatenate these units at appropriate positions. This resulted in intelligible and reasonably natural synthetic speech.

Intelligibility of synthetic speech also depends on selecting the units that match the target phonetic contexts. At times, the required phonetic context may not be available in the database. In such case, we propose that similar phones that are perceptually indistinguishable may replace these phonetic contexts. The most confused pairs of Tamil phones, which can be replaced by each other in specific contexts at the time of synthesis (if they are not available in the corpus) are found. Explorative experiments to determine the applicability of incorporating these techniques resulted in high mean opinion scores for the synthesized output from the native Tamil evaluators. Hence, we consider that this possibility of replacing missing phonetic contexts can be used in practical TTS.

Finally, when any person speaks the same sentence repeatedly, the speech waveforms don't have identical characteristics. With this motivation, the final portion of my research attempts to analyze the variability of characteristics of different instances of speech, when a speaker utters the same sentence multiple times, at different times. The idea is to look at the possibility of generating a slightly different synthetic speech each time the same text is synthesized, thus trying to make the TTS sound not monotonous and more human like.

Also, we observe that incorporating prosody and pause models for Indian language TTS would further enhance the synthetic speech quality output. These are some of the potential, unexplored areas ahead, for Indian speech synthesis.

Motivation for Bilingual TTS

In the present scenario, usage of English in Tamil text has become common and inevitable. If such words are omitted in TTS, the TTS would be less effective. Hence we have developed a bilingual Tamil TTS for generating Tamil and English by using the same synthesis Tamil data for both the languages. The sparsely occurring English text is converted into phonemes using a separate grapheme to phoneme converter and the corresponding phonemes are obtained from the available Tamil database for concatenation. The initial results are encouraging and we are working on some more improvements for better sounding English.

Tamil synthesis database has 5 hours of Tamil sentences recorded by a male professional Tamil speaker. The recorded database is rich in phonetic context and phonetic variations. The TTS takes Tamil Unicode input, and performs equivalent phonetic translation. In Tamil, some letters and phonetic contexts influence the phoneme of a letter, such as "ka" can become "ga" in some phonetic contexts. The rules for these phonetic changes are coded as rules in the grapheme to phoneme converter. The phonemes are then again grouped into polyphonic cluster. The clusters are searched in database to find a best choice is selected for a given context. We have developed a prosody based unit selection algorithm to further enhance the best selection for a given text.

Features/Specifications of the TTS

1. Unlimited Vocabulary : Any sentence involving any combination of native words of Tamil (or Kannada) is handled.
2. Quality : The intelligibility of the TTS is quite high, and it is also acceptably natural.
3. Text Encoding: Only text entered in Unicode will be handled. Other proprietary or public font encodings are not handled, and will not be handled, even in the future.

4. Web Demo: The TTS has been made available as a web demo. Go to the link, http://mile.ee.iisc.ernet.in:8080/tts_demo. The TTS demo page can be seen and a box, where the Tamil or Kannada text in Unicode must be submitted.
5. Test Input to the TTS: If you want to submit your own custom text input, you can do so, by typing using our open source Multilingual Indic keyboard interface: பன்மொழி வாயில் ishwavaangmukha), which you can download from http://code.google.com/p/indic-keyboards
6. Output Format: The TTS outputs a standard .wav file.
7. Testing: The web demo of Tamil TTS has now been tested by hundreds of people from around the world, and many GB's of synthesized. Wav files have been downloaded by them.

Current Limitations

It cannot handle numerals, proper nouns and words originating outside the current language handled by the TTS, sentences needing intonations changes, such as interrogative and exclamatory sentences. There may also be some mispronunciations at times. In the case of long sentences, even the pauses (phrase breaks) may not be at the instances, where a human speaker will naturally pause for better intelligibility and clarity.

Future Enhancement

All the current limitations mentioned above are being addressed by us, and will be updated in time. The numeral handling facility will be added very soon. Some of the causes for mispronunciations have been identified, and will be corrected next. However, further enhancement of naturalness requires significant research in computational linguistics and prosody and hence, may take considerable time to reach good quality.

Conclusion

MILE Laboratory has teamed up with Bookshare.org, an International non-profit organization, to provide Tamil and Kannada digital books (copyright free or permitted by authors) online to print-disabled people (visually challenged, old people with vision disabilities and people with other disabilities that make it impossible for holding a book and turn pages of it). The MILE OCRs and TTS in the respective language (Thirukkural/Vak) will be used for this purpose, and thus the printed content can directly be heard as speech on a desktop computer or laptop.

Acknowledgment

The TTSs were developed as part of a Research Project, funded by Ministry of Social Justice and Empowerment (MSJE), Government of India. The author also thanks Karthigeyan, Jayavardhana Rama, Prathibha, Muralishankar, Lakshmish Koushik, Parthasarathy, Arun, Abhinav, Vikram, Shivakumar and others, who contributed to the TTS research and development over a period of time.

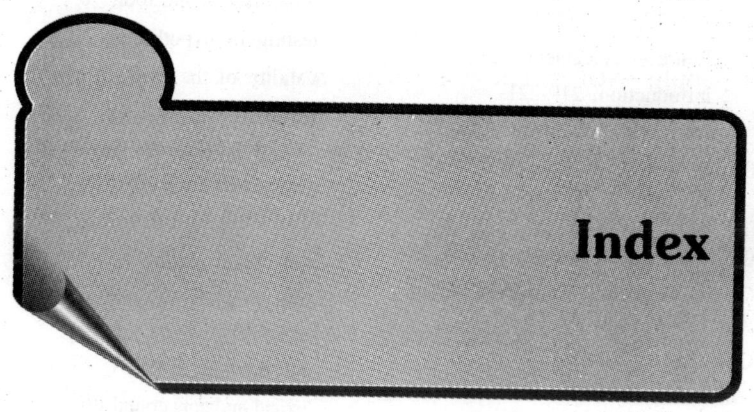

Index

A

Abhinava, 219

Anand Kumar, M., 98

Animated sangathamizh poems, 152-157

- advantages, 156
- how to implement, 155-156
- introduction, 152
- revival, 154-155
- sangathamizh literature, 153-154
- Tamil, 152-153
- why sangathamizh poems, 155

Arulmozi, S., 158

Automated processing of census forms in Tamil, 200-210

- additional features, 205-207
- architecture of system, 203-204
- common interface framework, 204
- data collection, 202-203
- error correction measures, 207-208
- introduction, 201-202
- pre-processing, 205
- results and discussions, 208-209

Autonomous Technology-Assisted Language Learning (ATALL), 14

B

Balaji, S., 44

Balasubramanian, N., 59

Beacon Primary School, 2

Belhe, Swapnil, 200

Big Books and Interactive White Board, 4

Bilingual TTS for Tamil and English, 219-224
- current limitations, 223
- features/specifications of the TTS, 222-223
- future enhancement, 223
- introduction, 219-221
- motivation for bilingual TTS, 222

British National Corpus (BNC), 187

C

California Tamil Academy (CTA), 26

Centre, State and Confederation of Indian Industry, 50

China, 61

Christmas, 34

Computational approaches for learning inflections in Tamil, 120-129
- feature extraction, 127-128
- introduction, 121-122
- neural network, 126-127
- related works, 122-123
- results and discussions, 128
- Tamil morphology, 123-126

Computer aided learning in Tamil sentences, 67-74
- construction of tool, 69
- data analysis, 71
- data collection, 70
- delimitations of the study, 68-69
- educational implications, 73
- findings, 73
- hypotheses of the study, 68
- introduction, 67
- methodology, 69
- objectives of the study, 68
- pilot study, 69-70
- procedure of the study, 70
- reliability of the tool, 70
- testing of hypotheses, 71-72
- validity of the tool, 70
- variables, 68

Conceptual lexicon for knowledge representation, 130-141
- abstraction and definition, 133
- conceptual graphs, 131-132
- conceptual representation, 135-137
- introduction, 130-131
- lexical and conceptual structures, 138-139
- prototype, 134
- schemata, 133-134
- semantic net work, 132
- why conceptual lexicon, 131

Context based information search for Thirukural, 114-119
- how the search engine works, 117-118
- introduction, 115
- literature survey, 115-116
- term weightage formula, 118

Creative Commons License, 62

D

Deterministic Finite State Automata (DFA), 147

Devi, Sobha Lalitha, 142

District Primary Education Programme, 45

E

Enhancing activity based Tamil teaching and learning using online video repositories, 52-58
- introduction, 53-54
- review of literature, 54
- using data mining techniques to enhance teaching and learning, 55-57
- using short video for lecture/demo, 54-55

Enhancing learning of Tamil language in a one-to-one computing environment, 1-12
- discussions of findings, 8
  - authentic activities, 8
  - feedback from parents, 9
  - learning abilities, 9
  - learning with technology-creation of digital stories, 9-10
  - pupils engagement and behaviour, 8-9
- introduction and purpose, 2
- issues and challenges, 10
  - pupil ICT readiness, 10-11
  - school infrastructure and support, 11
- pupils and parents surveys and interview, 7
- rationale, approach and design, 3-6
- research methods, 6
- research methods: pupils performance, 6-7
- teacher reflection notes and observations, 7

F

Face Generator, 113

FaceWaves, 106-113
- background, 108
- facewaves framework, 108
  - information system, 108-109
  - interface manager, 110
  - language tools, 109
  - wave processor, 109-110
- introduction, 107
- results, 111-113
- text to video subsystem, 110-111

From classical Tamil to computational Tamil, 184-191
- annotated corpora, 189 annotation standards, 190
- creation of data with community-wide participation, 190-191
- introduction and motivation, 185-187
- linguistic corpora to be developed, 187
- linguistic resources, 190
- multilingual corpora, 189
- national efforts on linguistic corpora, 187-189
- need for linguistic corpora, 191
- standards organizations, 190

G

Ganesan, M., 120

Geetha, T.V., 106

Government of India, 59

Government of Tamil Nadu, 57

H

Halloween, 34

Human Resource Development Department, 46

I

ICT for Tamil education in Tamil Nadu current challenges and opportunities, 44-51

basic requirements in using our Microsoft powerpoint models, 47-49

challenges ahead, 46-47

driving forces, 45

government initiatives and pathway, 49-50

impact of ICT, 45-46

introduction, 44

pathway for opportunities, 47

ICT tools, 11

Ilakiyaselvan, N., 114

Indian Union Territory of Puducherry, 44

Indira Gandhi National Open University (IGNOU), 38

Infocomm Development Authority (IDA), 2

Information Communication Technologies (ICT), 2

Information Retrieval, 116, 159

Information Technology, 37

Internet, 56

J

Jacob Ballas Children Garden (Singapore Botanical Gardens), 8

K

Karky, Madhan, 106

Kendriya Vidyalayas and Navodaya Vidyalayas, 50

Kiran, Shashi, 200

Kumaran, A., 184

L

Lakshmi, Seetha, 13

M

Malaysia, 44

Menon, A.G., 211

Meyyappan, Ilango, 26

Microsoft Power Point, 10

Ministry of Education, 2

Moodle, 75-83

add-on, 82-83

automatic, 82

course completion, 82

curriculum management, 76

curriculum management, 81

features, 83

how can it bring a difference, 77-78

introduction, 75

learning effectiveness, 76

management the flow between constituents of a course, 80

manual, 82

mapping the learning curve, 79-80

necessity, 82

providing a statistics on what is happening around him, 80

roles, 82

solution, 80
statistics, 83
tool for Tamil teaching, 90-97
activities, 94-95
administration and security, 95
introduction, 91-93
methodology, 95-96
other collaborative features, 95
recent developments, 96
reporting and monitoring, 95
teaching and learning through moodle, 93-94
what do I gain on reading further, 75-76
what is an LMS, 76-77
why do we need an LMS for learning Tamil language, 77
why moodle, 78-79
Morphological generator for Tamil, 98-105
algorithm developed for morphological generator, 101-102
creation of inflection table, 100-101
introduction, 99
methodology, 102-104
Mother Tongue, 2

N

Nagarajan, V., 90
Natarajan, Arul, 152
National Institute of Education, 13, 20
National Knowledge Commission, 59
National Mission for Education, 50
Natural Language Processing (NLP), 62, 99
Newport Asia Pacific University (NAPU), 38
Nirmala Devi, S., 36
Noun phrase chunker using finite state automata for an agglutinative language, 142-151
introduction, 142-144
description about the language, 144
noun phrases in Tamil, 144-146
Tamil NP chunker, 146-148
preprocessing works, 148
process in finite state automata, 148-149
results and discussion, 149-150

O

Open educational resources in the context of teaching and learning of Tamil as the first language, 59-66
challenges to the growing OER movement, 61-62
computerized question banks and online testing, 65
e-mail as a tool for teaching a language, 64
introduction, 59-60
mapping OERs, 61
multimedia and author ware, 63-64
natural language processing and language learning and teaching, 62-63

open educational researches, 60
software for teaching of reading and writing, 63
users and producers of OER, 61
Open Source Learning Management Software, 93

P

Panchayat Union Primary School, 69
Pattern based English, 211-218
introduction, 211-212
lexicalization, 215-216
parsing, 212
pattern based reordering, 212-214
reordering algorithm, 214
synthesizer, 216-217
testing and results, 217
transliteration, 216
Pillai, Anitha S., 192
Pokkisham, 23
Pongal, 34

Q

Quality analysis of Tamil virtual university, 84-89
mission, 86-88
objectives of the analysis, 86
QFD can be used to analyse the TVU such as, 85
steps in QFD in TVU, 88
thus the Tamil virtual university encloses, 85-86
TVU planning, 88-89

R

Rajan, K., 120
Rajendran, S., 98, 130
Rajeswari, T., 36
Rajkumar, S., 84
Ramakrishnan, AG, 200, 219
Ramalingam, V., 120
Ranjit, P., 52
Rekha, R.U., 98
Representation of kinship in WorldNet, 158-169
construction of synsets, 161-162
introduction, 159
kinship in WorldNet, 162-163
lexicographical concerns, 162
problems in creating synsets involving kinship relations, 163-167
word net, 159-161
Rituraj, 200
Rolc of regular expression in morphological analysis, 170-173
introduction, 170-171
levels in morphological analysis, 172
role of regular expression in affix stripping, 172-173
morphophonemic section, 173
root checking, 172

S

Sangathamizh poems, 152-157
Saravanan, S., 211
Saravanan, V., 52
Sarveswaran, K., 90
Shanmugam, R., 170
Shiva Kumar, H.R., 219
Singaravelu, G., 67

SMART schools, 50
Soman, Dhanalakshmi V., 98
Soman, K., 211
Somasundaram, Ravishankar, 75
Spell checker for Tamil using finite state automata, 192-199
  checking of words, 196
  finite state automaton, 194-195
  introduction to spell checking, 193-194
  representation of words using finite state automaton, 195-196
  Sandhi checker, 197
  suggestions, 197-198
  word not recognized by finite state automaton, 196-197
Sri Lanka, 23, 44
Srinivasan, S., 174
Study on the role of Tamil virtual university in Tamil-teaching and learning at elementary level, 36-43
  analysis of data, 39
  changing role of the teacher, 37
  educational implications of the study, 40
  findings of the study, 40
  importance of teachers, 37
  introduction, 36
  method and procedure, 39
  need for technology, 38
  need for the study, 37
  objectives of the study, 39
  sample, 39
  Tamil virtual university, 38
  technology and education, 36
  tool, 39
Sundaram, Suresh, 200

T

Tamil New Year, 34
Tamil Virtual University, 37
Teaching and resource building in teacher education, 13-25
  constructing knowledge, 23
  current development, 22-23
  interactivity, 23-24
  introduction, 14-17
  PB works in Tamil resource bank, 17-19, 21
  preparation process, 19-20
  preparation process teaching writing through IT for dip Ed II class, 20-21
Thanksgiving, 34
The Webolution, 75
Thirukural, 114-119
Transliteration schemes for Tamil to roman and roman to Tamil characters, 174-183
  introduction, 174
  Tamil keyboard layout, 174-175
  Tamil-to-roman transliteration, 175-179
  roman-to-Tamil transliteration, 180-182
  applications, 182

U

UNESCO Forum in 2002, 60
United States, 54

Use of technology in running a Tamil school in USA, 26-35
annual day, 34
communication, 33
CTA history, 27
CTA objectives, 27
high school credit program, 33-34
introduction, 26-27
multimedia in syllabus, 33
school profile, 29
student performance, 30-32
student registration, 29-30
Tamil virtual university, 34-35
use of technology, 27
user profiles, 28-29

V

Varman, Ravi, 106
Vijay Sundar Ram, R., 142
Vikram, L.R., 219
Vivekanandan, K., 52

W

Word Sense Disambiguation, 159

Y

Yashwntrao Chavan Maharastra Open University, 38